RAM CHARAN AND **RAJ B. VATTIKUTI**

THE DIGITAL LEADER

FINDING A FASTER,
MORE PROFITABLE PATH TO
EXCEPTIONAL GROWTH

WILEY

Published by John Wiley & Sons, Inc., Hoboken, New Jersey.
Published simultaneously in Canada.

For general information on our other products and services or for technical support, please contact our Customer Care Department within the United States at (800) 762-2974, outside the United States at (317) 572-3993 or fax (317) 572-4002.

Wiley publishes in a variety of print and electronic formats and by print-on-demand. Some material included with standard print versions of this book may not be included in e-books or in print-on-demand. If this book refers to media such as a CD or DVD that is not included in the version you purchased, you may download this material at http://booksupport.wiley.com. For more information about Wiley products, visit www.wiley.com.

Library of Congress Cataloging-in-Publication Data is available:

ISBN 9781119900085 (Hardback)
ISBN 9781119900108 (ePDF)
ISBN 9781119900092 (ePub)

Cover Design: Wiley
Cover Image: © nadla/Getty Images

SKY10034443_051222

*Dedicated to the hearts and souls of the joint
family of twelve siblings and cousins living under one
roof for fifty years, whose personal sacrifices made my formal
education possible.*

—Ram Charan

*This book is dedicated to the practitioners who drive digital
business change; your dedication is an inspiration.*

—Raj B. Vattikuti

Contents

Acknowledgments   *vii*

PART ONE   **1**

1 The New and Simpler Path to Digitalize
   Your Business   **3**

2 Taking the First Bite   **11**

3 Getting Started   **19**

4 The <u>Right</u> First Step   **33**

5 Launch!   **47**

6 From Algorithms to New Models   **61**

7 What Can Go Wrong and How to Make
   It Right   **67**

PART TWO   **79**

8 Low Investment, High Impact Digital Business
   Themes: Use Cases   **81**

About the Authors   *149*

Acknowledgments

The ever-changing nature of technology and the proliferation of data has been the catalyst for the extraordinary growth in the demand for digital business. Companies are literally reinventing themselves at an increasing rate and frequency. Those companies that embrace this new paradigm will find success; those that don't will fall further and further behind.

We want to thank the practitioners who contributed to this book. They understand that companies are dealing with complex challenges and struggle to implement needed change on their own digital journey. They are industry experts working with companies across the globe helping to simplify business and technologies that bring speed, scale, and outcomes. We created this digital playbook to provide the guidance, approach, and real-world examples to help others achieve success in their own digital business transformation.

A special thanks to Anil Allewar, Zoran Bogdanovic, Dennis Carey, Paras Chandaria, Badhrinath Kannan, Anuj Kaushik, Gautam Makani, Jayaprakash Nair, Jac Nasser, Raghu Potini, Ignacio Segovia, Minoj Singh, Anil Somani, Krishna Sudheendra, Raj Sundaresan, Vipul Valamjee, Srikanth Velamakanni, Sivanandam Venkatasamy, and George Zoghbi.

We also want to thank James Sterngold for turning our ideas into text, Geri Willigan for her contributions, and our editor Zach Schisgal and the Wiley team for their guiding hand throughout the process.

Part One

1

The New and Simpler Path to Digitalize Your Business

You've heard the dire warnings to companies that have yet to incorporate digital technology into their business. "Digitize or die" is shorthand for the simple truth that you cannot compete for long against companies that are using algorithms and machine learning when you are not. The other players will be better than you at understanding and delivering what customers want, better at pricing, better at widening their margins, and better at generating cash.

The imperative to digitize is clear, yet what we hear in countless conversations with senior leaders of high-performing companies around the world is that adopting digital technology is too expensive, too disruptive, and takes too long. Some companies have spent tens if not hundreds of millions of dollars trying to become a so-called digital business with little to show for it; they are losing faith that the benefits will ever materialize.

Then there are others who still don't know how to start. Even mounting evidence that digital technology can take your company to great heights—as it has for some traditional businesses as well as start-ups—is often not enough to get a company to move.

The good news for laggards as well as those who are knee-deep in costly and frustrating efforts is that the technology industry itself has crossed the Rubicon. Making your company digital doesn't have to be a "big bang" that upends the entire organization at once or is a never-ending cash drain. It is now faster, cheaper, and easier than ever. It can be implemented in small pieces, each of which delivers measurable results that in turn can fund follow-up projects that are easily linked together.

This is newly possible because in the past few years, a cottage industry of small vendors has emerged that is taking advantage of advances in machine learning and artificial intelligence. Many of these vendors employ people who are not just technically astute but also have business savvy. They are highly skilled in providing the precise applications of ML and AI a client company needs to address its pain points. What they accomplish is not merely *digitizing* the business—meaning converting information into 1s and 0s—but *digitalizing* the business, meaning combining relevant data with algorithms designed to quickly deliver the critical business outcomes the company needs.

These developments make digitalization eminently doable. The amount of cash you need to get started is manageable for almost any company. And if you home in on the right places to start, the benefits will materialize much sooner than you think possible.

This new group of vendors—or digital enablers, as we have come to call them—are not well known, but they have track records of delivering cutting-edge technology for companies of all sizes. Even some of the digital giants, such as Amazon, have used their services. With the help of a digital enabler, a company can begin its digital journey in months, not years, at a cost closer to $400,000 than to $4 million, with measurable results in as short a time period as six months.

We have taken numerous clients on this journey. The anxious call we received one evening in August 2020, at the height of the Covid-19 pandemic, from the president of a large clothing retailer, is one example. The president explained that his stores in India were completely cut off from customers when the Indian economy went into lockdown. That had led to a domino effect—without a functioning website for e-commerce to replace the lack of in-store sales, inventory was backing up in stores and warehouses, crippling suppliers, and strangling revenues. Even worse, it's flagship high-growth brand was built on satisfying customers. Its inability to meet their needs meant customers might become disillusioned with the brand.

The next day, Ram contacted three of the best digital enablers he knew, and in consultation with the president agreed on one of them. He immediately called that firm's CEO and, within 72 hours, the vendor and the retailer had each assembled teams that would work together to plan and oversee the project. The digital vendor's team of data scientists, algorithm experts, and other software technicians flew to India to get their arms around the problem.

The following week the digital team presented its model for building a new digital platform to support the company's website and e-commerce in India and give its management easy access to data. Just four weeks later the vendor conducted a computer simulation of the new system to prove the concept. Five weeks after that, they had the system up and running.

The retailer came back to life in India, even as the pandemic persisted. Sales were unclogged, cash flow recovered, and the company was energized to plan for the next steps in creating a fully digitalized business.

This example and others like it give you every reason to be optimistic. We have seen digital enablers complete projects of similar scope in a range of businesses—health care, banking, agriculture, and others—with similarly low costs and fast tangible returns. We are convinced that for a vast majority of companies, using outside help to take on bite-size projects one after another is the best way to digitalize a business.

The ultimate goal of digitalization is the same as ever: to tap the immense potential of digital technology to transform nearly everything about your business, from its business model and money-making to its customer relationships, supply chain, and organizational structure. Digital technology can change how you gather information, how you design products, how you make decisions, how you shape your value chain end-to-end, and how you understand and delight your customers.

Such powerful changes require imagination along with technology. Merely plugging in the latest digital tools does not accomplish the same thing. Even if you tackle a digital project to solve an immediate problem, as was the case at the retailer, it should be seen as an opportunity to rethink a part of your business, and it will suggest opportunities to improve other aspects of the business next.

This book explains our way of thinking about how to move forward in digitalizing your business by taking small steps that yield observable, measurable results in the near term. Think of the book as a lantern shining a light on the path that will take you from digital laggard to digital leader. We explain how to pinpoint projects that are bite-size and in synch with your highest business priorities and show how digital enablers who straddle the technology and practitioner worlds can help define them. We will introduce you to a number of these digital enablers and explain how to find and evaluate the right ones for your business and how best to work with them.

Over time the benefits of digitalizing one part of your business at a time will build on each other, and the impact will compound. The technology is not the change; what your leadership does with the technology, the process of experimentation and continuous innovation, is what generates the dramatic change.

Data is a fundamental part of any digitalization effort because the output of any algorithm depends crucially on the quality and relevance of the data that is run through it. Even sophisticated algorithms from Google Analytics or IBM's Watson cannot generate useful insights if the data is incomplete. In most organizations, data is scattered, hidden, and in various formats. It must be gathered and converted into a consistent format so that it is the same for anyone in the organization who is authorized to access it. A digital enabler can turn data into a "single source of truth" that is both useful and unifying. Shared access to common data drives out politicking and fosters collaboration and speed. Giving it to decision makers is like giving a person with poor vision a perfect pair of glasses; they will see the ramifications of their choices with exceptional clarity.

As enormous volumes of data flow through your operations, from suppliers, vendors, warehouses, and customers, you can, with AI, turn that information into actionable items, such as personalized pricing based on analysis of individuals' consumption patterns. You will understand your customers as never before and be able to create new products in record time with significantly lower risk of failure. You can conserve cash by matching sales forecasts and suppliers seamlessly.

Otherwise unthinkable organizational changes also become possible, such as eliminating all but three hierarchical layers and customizing career paths to an individual's particular talent. Done right, digitalization produces visible successes that solve vexing business problems and energize the company. People become eager for the next project, not afraid of it, an aspect of this approach that should not be undervalued.

If you've not yet made a commitment to start digitalizing your company, you're not alone. Some 90 percent of companies have been wavering. In addition, a McKinsey partner once told us that as many as 70 percent of those that tried to build digital businesses failed in their efforts. A recent study by Forrester Consulting confirmed this reality and added that the best corporate decision makers understood that successful efforts in creating a digital business required constant attention and improvement to reap the very substantial benefits. This is not a one-and-done exercise.

Another recent analysis quantified at least some of the benefits. The analysis, by the Connected Commerce Council, Google, and Greenberg, Inc., found that digitally advanced small businesses retained customers more than three times better than "digitally uncertain businesses," those that had failed to deploy the full suite of digital tools, and the advanced businesses acquired new customers at a rate of 20 times better than the digital laggards. This is your lifeblood!

You should recognize that the equation has changed. Forces have converged to make the risk of stumbling far lower than the risk of standing still. Success is well within your reach.

What will be your first bite?

2

Taking the First Bite

What can the first "bite" in making a digital business actually achieve? Here's what several pioneers found in successfully tackling different parts of their value chain.

Turning a Chaotic Data Flow into a Single Source of Truth for Sharper Strategies

For Coca-Cola HBC, a sprawling Coca-Cola bottler based in Switzerland, the issue was a lack of visibility into various parts of the organization, which made it hard to gauge relative performance and identify the best opportunities for growth. The company needed to build a complete, granular data system providing a holistic view of the company's far-flung operations, what we call a single source of truth. The question was not just how to create a platform to assemble a large flow of data in one place but how to deploy digital tools that could quickly deliver insights leaders could use to improve their decision making on things such as capital allocation.

Coca-Cola HBC is a data-rich, highly complex business. It operates in 28 countries across three continents, from Ireland to Eastern Russia and south to Nigeria, regions filled with growing wealth and promise. But during a dinner I was having with Zoran Bogdanovic, the CEO, he mentioned his deep frustration over the kind of data that he and his leadership team had access to. It was not centrally organized, so it came in different formats and followed different standards. It did not necessarily measure the same things in the same way in different markets, and it was not available in a format that gave executives a full picture, with easy comparisons between markets, in real time. Worse, it was organized into disconnected silos, which some senior executives jealously guarded, obscuring the big picture.

The unfortunate result was that different executives with different responsibilities held differing and sometimes conflicting information. That meant, of course, that they had conflicting perspectives on strategic priorities. Data had become a weapon to be protected and held close, not a resource to be shared for developing unified strategies.

One result was that the executives, including the CEO, did not always trust the data they received, which led to arguments on the company's strategies and unnecessary diversions. Which region should get new investment? What areas would be cut back? When should they introduce new products and where? Which customers offered the best growth opportunities? It was difficult to address these critical strategic questions without the leadership speaking the same language based on common data inputs. That reality prevented the senior executives from grasping the best opportunities for growth in real time, inhibiting value creation.

Zoran explained that the company enjoyed solid market shares in its regions but realized feeble revenue growth, holding back its substantial potential. It was not able to deploy coordinated, end-to-end strategies that leveraged the large volumes of valuable customer data it received every day, which it needed to allow the company to engage seamlessly with its customers, suppliers, and staff and expand recurring revenues.

This is not an unusual problem. Most likely you either have this problem now or have had to tackle it in the past. What we know is that the solution is not nearly as difficult, expensive, or disruptive as many suppose.

Zoran and his team needed to take essential steps to create a digital business, beginning with deploying digital tools to organize the company's huge data flows into a single source of truth, across silos and geographies, digested, harmonized, and analyzed with the help of algorithms and AI. The data and its analysis would be available on a central platform, or dashboard, designed with visualization tools to make information easy to grasp.

It was essential that the same data would be visible to a broad range of authorized executives, no matter their geographies or places in the corporate hierarchy, and continuously available in real time 24/7 at the stroke of a few computer keys.

We connected the company with Fractal Analytics, a digital builder that has worked with major corporations from Visa and Philips to P&G and Wells Fargo. Experienced and intensely focused, Fractal hammered out a plan that began with immersive sessions with the end users of the company's systems. That produced a more precise problem statement and understanding of the needs of the new platform.

Fractal synthesized this information and was able to draw up a map of all the company's data stories and how they flowed and needed to come together and to define the journey from data input to decisions. With that start, Fractal quickly built a platform to collect and process all the incoming data from the many regions and parts of the company, all of which was entered into a unified system with seamless integration.

Quick access to common metrics across the business accelerated decision making and assisted in setting data-driven priorities for the company as a whole. It allowed advanced data analytics to be applied across the entire value chain. It altered, in the process, the mindset of the leadership toward a more data-driven, collaborative model. Fractal also helped with execution sponsorship, providing product champions to ensure implementation and ownership of the platform. The time required to design the prototype? Just 10 weeks.

Improving Demand Forecasts

An Indian agricultural company that produces chemicals such as pesticides, fungicides, and crop growth regulators traditionally relied on its sales teams and territory managers to provide forecasts of demand for their products and used those to plan manufacturing. But agriculture can be influenced by an immense number of variables, from the weather and consumer preferences to government policies, which can change quickly over time, and the agriculture company's leaders were frustrated by historically inaccurate projections that threw manufacturing schedules off and created costly errors.

Those inaccurate forecasts produced manufacturing plans that were as much as 50 percent off. When the forecasts were too low, it meant the company was missing sales opportunities due to underproduction; that was true with 20 percent of its products. When they were too high, the case with 80 percent of its products, it suffered costly wastage. The poor assimilation and analysis of data affected suppliers and customers. The solution was to collect all the data that could affect farming decisions, from numerous sources, tracked over time, correlated and assessed with AI and algorithms to discern patterns and make precision forecasts.

A digital enabler, Altimetrik Corp., created a vast digital agricultural data collection system across India, utilizing an array of important measures, such as crop planting patterns, plant diseases, consumption patterns, rainfall, and government farming policies. The new platform assembled the data, harmonized it so analysis and comparisons could be made in real time, identified historical patterns and correlations, and used predictive analysis to project key metrics. That was the foundation of their single source of truth.

Assembling this data and further analyzing it with AI and machine learning provided new insights and data-driven accuracy. This generated far more reliable demand forecasts and gave the company a far deeper understanding of trends and its customers' needs. This data-driven approach not only removed the drag on their bottom line from incorrect production runs, it allowed them to develop more competitive pricing.

The digital system reduced forecasting deviations by up to 80 percent. The effort, focused on 15 products, was completed in six weeks.

Making the Essential Leap into E-Commerce—In 12 Weeks

For most retail businesses, e-commerce is a necessity, not an option. The pioneering success of retailers such as Amazon, and the impact of the pandemic lockdowns, are radically altering what consumers expect and what retailers must deliver to maintain their loyalty and sustain brand growth.

Sophisticated online ordering systems, real-time status updates, intensive inventory management, and quick and easy home delivery require extremely complex systems that must mesh seamlessly and that, for companies that make the transition, must be operational in weeks. Egen is a digital enabler that has mastered a replicable, end-to-end process for constructing digital businesses, including the order and delivery process.

Egen's turnkey e-commerce systems have been developed to go operational typically in 12 weeks. Its four-step process includes setting up the digital product ordering process with real-time responses confirming availability of products, inventory controls, and delivery schedules. The system must be able to interact harmoniously in real time with the numerous other digital systems being employed by customers, suppliers, warehouses, logistics operations, payment processing, fraud detection, and delivery teams.

Layered on top are algorithms and machine learning capabilities to spot shifting market and product trends and customer purchasing patterns to deliver better inventory forecasting for the retailer and useful purchase recommendations and product ideas for consumers—in minutes rather than days or weeks.

The benefits? Often these include 15–20 percent revenue growth and cost reductions of as much as 30 percent as redundant operations are weeded out. These are the results you can expect.

Where will you begin?

3

Getting Started

Turning your company into a digital business—without harming your legacy business—is not simply a matter of unleashing the software engineers and their algorithms and waiting for them to flip the "on" switch. Placing your company on digital platforms and creating the single source of truth affects your company's structure, its culture, its priorities, its decision-making speed, and its opportunities. In other words, it fundamentally influences vision and leadership.

Technology makes it possible to create digital businesses, but your people create true transformation. "Digital transformation" has become a buzzword. What we will explain is that the real performance benefits come when you and your team take ownership of the new systems and the new way of thinking about and managing your business.

Chief Executive magazine joined forces with Amazon Web Services in mid-2021 to conduct a survey of how CEOs were navigating the process of building digital businesses, and it made a sobering finding about CEO attitudes: "Becoming a more digitally sophisticated enterprise is essential, and they are struggling to make it happen." Nearly half of the leaders surveyed said that they are just "hanging in there" in the process of creating a digitally innovative business, or, as some admitted, they are "out of their depth."

What issues were inhibiting the transformation? The problems all reflected on leadership: 38 percent said it was due to not having the right talent, 24 percent cited a failure to prioritize the digital process, and 21 percent said the corporate culture stood in the way, according to the survey.

If that surprises you, it shouldn't. Change is never easy. But it does underscore a critical element in your digital journey—making certain you get the people part of the equation right before you even begin. The critical preparatory step in successfully launching your transformation requires putting in place the right leadership team to drive the effort. Getting this initial step wrong could hobble the effort. We have long believed that talent is the single most important determinant of a company's success. "People before strategy" is the phrase Ram often repeats in working with business executives. "People before digitalization" is a variation on that theme.

We urge you to think long and hard about leadership before you even begin to approach digital enablers to help with the creation of digital platforms, the single source of truth, and a digital business. The top executive talent, technical talent, and business experts you select to drive your process must form a collaborative team that will set priorities, choose the first bite-size part of the project, work closely with and guide the digital enabler, and push implementation down into your organization. Remember, this is not a "technology upgrade." It begins the creation of a new digital business.

Each member of the team must be carefully selected for their specific capabilities and perspectives on how your business will create and develop its new opportunities. The right combination of leadership and expertise is key to opening the aperture to nonlinear growth and ensuring that rigid organizational boundaries, always a stumbling block, do not prevent you from realizing entirely new levels of performance and defining a new future.

Eventually many people in the company will be involved in the project, but the critical vision and guidance must come from a small, fully committed group that understands what is at stake and is capable of taking the practical steps that will push you forward quickly and communicate how the new processes will work. What follows are guidelines for choosing *who* should drive your digital journey, and how they can prepare themselves for this important leadership challenge.

Leadership from the Very Top

We know that business leaders are busy people with enormous demands on their time—Raj himself is the executive chairman of the digital enabler Altimetrik, and Ram circles the globe in restless cycles to meet with his CEO and senior executive clients. Still, we want to be unequivocal in saying that, in most cases, the CEO should personally lead the effort to create a digital business. Of course, the job can be successfully delegated at times, but even then, it should be to another C-suite executive with a deep understanding of the business, and the CEO needs both to monitor and be deeply engaged with the process, visibly so.

The CEO will not be the sole decision maker, but his or her direct involvement and implicit endorsement of the process is critical for several reasons: the chief executive knows better than anyone what the business's real priorities are or should be, has ultimate control of the allocation of resources, and critically, has the power to break through any organizational roadblocks to building an effective digital strategy. Not least, the very presence of the CEO establishes that the digital business is a top strategic priority and that everyone needs to get on board and participate.

At Singapore-based DBS Group, the largest bank by assets in Southeast Asia, the CEO, Piyush Gupta, led the successful effort to transform what was a traditional bank, starting with his arrival at the bank in 2009, into a fintech company with a high-performance digital platform capable of competing with digital-born financial institutions. In recognition of this transformation and the leveraging of digital technology, *Euromoney* magazine named DBS Group the "World's Best Digital Bank"—twice—and, in 2019, *Harvard Business Review* called the bank one of the top ten most transformative organizations of the decade.

In a 2021 article, the *MIT Sloan Management Review* cited Gupta's personal leadership in this reimagining of the bank. "Gupta's efforts and personal passions—and his willingness to push the bank to experiment, even when it might result in short-term failure—powerfully illustrate a senior executive's ability to lead the effective adoption of a new technology," the magazine article said.

One of the purposes of pursuing the digital process sequentially, tackling one bite-size piece of the business at a time, is that completion of each of these steps should deliver concrete performance enhancements in a relatively short time frame, supporting the overarching business strategy—without disrupting your legacy moneymaking capabilities—and building the organization's confidence to do more.

No one has a better feel for the overall business objectives and the relative importance of each piece in contributing to key goals than the CEO. He or she will know better than anyone how new sources of revenue, increased margins, radically lower costs, new product development, and swifter decision making can help realize these objectives and create value.

Building that digital business will change how work gets done for at least some subset of employees. It is not a mere technological upgrade of existing processes, an efficiency measure. Some people will be energized by the performance enhancements and new possibilities. Others, however, may be intimidated by the new tools or threatened by changes in their jobs and new collaborative work patterns. The CEO's continual communication and assurances are key to overcoming such inevitable organizational resistance.

Even as we stress the need for the CEO taking the lead and urge him or her to carve out the time to do so, we have seen situations where constraints on the CEO's time made that arrangement impractical. In such cases, another leader close to the CEO can take charge as a representative of the business leadership because this is a business process, not a mere technology process.

Our experience underscores that such a digital "czar" should be accessible to the CEO, perhaps someone who works on the same floor. It should be someone who is deeply engaged with operations, has demonstrated business savvy, and knows the business inside and out and, therefore, has a lot of credibility throughout the organization. He or she need not be an expert on digital technology (more on that later in this chapter) but should at least have a deep appreciation for the power of the technological tools you are deploying. This person may be someone in the line of succession, or in the second tier, and this is likely to be their full-time responsibility for the duration of the process.

At BMW, Harald Krueger, the company head, led the digital business effort. At an energy company based in India, the second in command led the digital effort because the CEO had to concentrate his efforts on executing a series of acquisitions. Again, the chosen leader is likely to be assigned to the position full time and report directly to the CEO.

Removing the person from their regular job might raise concerns about who will perform the functions of the old position, and, of course, it may raise questions to some of whether it is a one-way ticket out of the old leadership structure. Those concerns can be quelled by the CEO's assuring this person that the new assignment is pivotal to the company's future and will advance, not harm, his or her career.

In any case, the CEO must stay involved and should get detailed reports at least every two weeks. Frequent communication will ensure that projects don't get bogged down or deviate from their intended focus. In one case, the CEO worked with the vendor to help define the initial project—to create the capacity to gather and analyze customer data—and then delegated supervision to his CFO. The project soon morphed into something entirely different and less useful: using existing systems to analyze existing data. When the CEO realized what was happening, he again took charge.

But remember that even though this is a transformation that relies on the development and application of excellent technology, it is fundamentally not about AI or algorithms—it is about reinventing your business and accelerating the creation of value with a single source of truth and a more collaborative culture focused on innovation.

Thus, while it may seem logical to delegate the building of your digital company to your CIO or CTO, in almost all cases that would be a big mistake. You are not requesting an IT fix-up. It is a job for those with business vision and hands-on experience in your most important business operations, working closely with others who understand what can be done with the algorithms, software, and data analytics.

The Right Kind of Technology Talent

Two different kinds of expertise are crucial to the success of any digital transformation: deep understanding of the business and deep expertise in software, AI, ML, and algorithms. There must be a close partnership that marries those two areas of expertise. The CEO, or the C-suite delegate, will bring the right business savvy to the job, but don't simply expect your current IT team to bring the appropriate technological expertise you need. This is an important distinction that you must take into account in formulating your action plan.

While some CTOs or CIOs are well informed and experienced with the newest digital and analytics technologies, many others have built their careers supporting the old SAP and ERP systems and the old mindset they represent. They are likely to be invested in your older technologies.

The new tools require a new type of vision and collaborative skills. However well intentioned, traditional IT experts may not fully appreciate these skills or have the time to learn them. They may have the desire to help, but if they have not mastered machine learning and are not familiar with how to get the most out of common algorithms, you can't afford the learning curve. There are plenty of examples of companies that put an IT executive on the digital team and ended up replacing them, losing valuable time.

It is common, then, to have to recruit a technology expert to work on the construction of your digital business. If you find it necessary to take this path, the new specialist should report directly to the CEO, not to the current head of IT, and they should function as a copilot on the team. If there are wounded feelings on the existing IT staff, the CEO will have to manage those.

If it appears you will be, in effect, creating two parallel IT departments, that may be inevitable. One will be needed to maintain and operate your legacy technology systems so normal business operations are not disrupted, and the other will be focused on applying the new digital technologies.

Starbucks began on this route in what is now its much-admired digital transformation when, in 2012, it appointed both a chief information officer and a chief digital officer, a process that eventually led to its far-sighted "Digital Flywheel" strategy to enhance the customer experience and apply AI to better serve customers and anticipate their needs.

The new hire, should you choose this path, will play a crucial role in determining how the business will build its future, and the selection process should reflect the high stakes. An ideal CDO will bring to the digital business team a good understanding of how to develop business-facing solutions, but he or she should also have a feel for the business or a willingness to learn about it. If they don't immediately demonstrate this kind of business knowledge, look for indications that they will develop it over time as they work in partnership with the CEO and other business leaders. Of course, you should also look at your existing staff, including at lower level, high-performing employees to identify the right talent for the job.

If you lack the resources to hire fresh talent with the necessary skills in AI and ML, you can often achieve your objectives by working with digital enablers who can work as partners. Asking the right questions, you can test for this before you engage them. But don't lose sight of the fact that you need a thoughtful technology expert involved in the discussions to explain what the technology is capable of and how it should be deployed, steps that will spur your team's creative thinking, one of your primary goals in undertaking this process.

Filling Out the Team

The CEO and an IT expert are core members of your digital team. A good start in sending everyone the right message on its objectives is to call it the "business transformation office," or "business creation office." But you will need a few other people to round it out. Your instinct may be to call on your direct reports, the CFO and COO, for example. But think instead about who will bring crucial observations, good business instincts, a willingness to embrace change, and imagination.

One truism in the digital era is that *every* company is ultimately a consumer company. Even if you are selling parts of parts, it is wise to know the needs and behavior of end users as well as the immediate customers. Many innovative applications of technology involve engaging directly with consumers and using the data to reimagine how you serve their needs.

So you should bring someone with knowledge of these consumers onto the team. This could be the marketing chief or someone more directly involved with the market space. Seniority doesn't matter. Often, the best ideas bubble up from lower levels of your business, where younger executives may be more closely involved in customer-facing activities. The person should be able to offer their observations, identify pain points in the business and value chain, and help imagine a new customer experience.

It will also be helpful to choose someone who is a leader of teams—someone who can keep the team on task and, importantly, bring other executives on board when the time comes to execute decisions. This person should have demonstrated knowledge of the organization and credibility with other leaders.

The exact composition and size of this close-in team will vary, but in our experience, four is often a very workable number. It provides a mix of viewpoints while allowing each member to express their ideas freely, an important consideration when brainstorming and getting feedback on untested ideas. Consider that many of today's digital giants got off the ground when three or four innovators put their heads together in a garage or a coffee shop and let the creative ideas flow.

Learning Up Front

The group's composition is important, but whether the CEO is directly leading this transformation or closely supervising it, he or she must be both a role model and active participant in another essential facet of the process: learning. The CEO must become a sort of chief algorithms officer and know enough about AI and data analytics to have meaningful discussions with the true technology experts, embrace their guidance, and incorporate that knowledge into his or her vision. Put simply, learning cannot be delegated.

CEOs and members of this top team must understand what algorithms and the single source of truth can do to open their minds to new possibilities, including enormous expansion of market value. Taking your business's huge flow of data and analyzing it with algorithms and AI will help you build predictive models of customer behavior and develop extraordinary new insights.

Andy Jassy, Amazon's new CEO, who built the company's cloud business, AWS, does not write software code. But he has always understood what the new digital technologies could do and saw how they could be applied in imaginative ways to the market needs he perceived. Jack Ma, founder of Alibaba, was not a technologist—he was an English teacher—but he worked closely with them so he could understand the best ways of applying those tools. You will eventually want many people throughout your organization to have this basic knowledge of technology, but educating the top team is essential.

Some simple algorithms are at the heart of many successful digital businesses. A matching algorithm, for example, is the basis for Uber and Lyft, as well as match.com. You could start by learning about the ten or so most common algorithms.

There are many ways to learn. One company in Boston sent its top team to a specially created program at MIT for one day a month, not to master new programming languages but to expose the business leaders to the tools and capabilities that are available. Another company had a computer science professor from a nearby college teach the team about algorithms and how they helped translate large volumes of data into usable insights.

Learning what other companies have done will help you grasp how quickly ML and AI can solve seemingly intractable problems. The stories in the previous chapter and throughout this book might inspire you, but so can conversations with leaders of companies that have used digital platforms in an innovative way. The digital business process is filled with uncertainties and can make some executives fearful, but time and again we have seen the anxiety lift when a leader visits another team and hears firsthand what they've been able to accomplish in a very short time.

As resistance falls and excitement builds, the question then is, what will you tackle first? We will walk you through that process.

4

The <u>Right</u> First Step

Li & Fung, based in Hong Kong, is a more than 100-year-old company that has built its business and strong reputation as a master at managing complex supply chains, operating between the world's major manufacturing hubs in East Asia and some of the world's leading Western brands. It works with these brands, such as Kohl's, its largest customer, Skechers, Hang Ten, and Sean John, in processing and filling production orders, supporting the design, materials sourcing, manufacturing, logistics, and delivery of consumer products, largely garments, in an end-to-end process.

But e-commerce, changing consumer habits, and drastically reduced manufacturing cycles are challenging its business. Despite its decades of experience and global network, it found itself struggling to keep up with the changes, which were squeezing cash flow and revenues. The company finally came to Altimetrik, an expert digital enabler, with problems that it was not able to resolve with its legacy systems. Its overly complex, incompatible order management systems simply weren't keeping up, and cash flow was suffering.

A key challenge the company faced was coordinating both ends of its value chain—on one side, there were an array of different brands, each with different manufacturing cycles, design and ordering systems, and accounts payment processes, and at the other end of its operations were the vendors and the factories that produced the products, with their own separate data systems and much shorter payment cycles. That created a growing financial mismatch, with overly long design and ordering systems delaying incoming cash flow from Li & Fung customers while the manufacturers had to be paid rapidly.

The company initiated a long-range planning exercise, but it needed to burrow in even further and rethink its day-to-day order processing and management process to coordinate the different ends of its value chain seamlessly and more effectively. That was the bottleneck squeezing cash flow.

In the very first meeting with Li & Fung, Altimetrik's engineers sought out and spoke with the customer-facing managers and quickly identified a specific pain point that was both a problem and an opportunity. Each brand that the company served had its own separate process for preparing and sending in orders, requiring laborious manual processing for Li & Fung. There was no standardization. Even within the systems of each client company there were often different, incompatible information formats employed for the different sections of the design and ordering process. That created much duplication, with no uniform system for order entry, design, or processing. Each brand used a different system for the specifications, different software and formats, and a different means for correcting errors.

That, Altimetrik realized, was the right bite-size piece of Li & Fung's operations that ought to be addressed first. The overarching solution was simplification of the various sources of information and its processing, creating a powerful single source of truth.

Altimetrik helped Li & Fung build a new digital business system that applied a common format to the entire order entry and processing system. Machine learning and artificial intelligence processes were deployed to gather and organize the incoming orders, standardize the information, and autocorrect any apparent anomalies. The data was entered into a unified portal and converted into an essential single source of truth, accessible on one standardized visual platform. Taking control over what had been a chaotic and uneven inflow of design and order data ultimately reduced the processing cycle to a matter of days rather than weeks, a significant improvement.

In addition, with less time needed for handling each order, Li & Fung staff had more time for collaborating with the customers on design details and resolving any day-to-day problems more rapidly, enhancing collaborative relationships. Cash flow improved quickly as a result. The platform and its single source of truth not only lowered costs, it improved accuracy and shortened the cycle time. Importantly, the CEO now could determine the value proposition each customer presented and make decisions based on this improved understanding.

Instead of meeting resistance to the proposed solution, Altimetrik won support by working side by side with Li & Fung employees to understand the heart of their business problem. Solving it quickly to make their life easier boosted confidence and motivation to use technology more.

That experience is a reminder that, as the old saying goes, a journey of a thousand miles begins with a single step. What we can add to that adage is that the key to a successful digital journey is taking the *right* first step and building on that progress to support a self-reinforcing digital transformation process. Particularly in a fast-moving economy, getting that first step right is critical for delivering quick results, demonstrating the benefits of transformation into a digital business, and getting employee buy-in.

Our experience has demonstrated not just the power of this truth but how badly things can go wrong if that first step is poorly chosen or if the company tries to skip ahead and undertake a "big bang" approach to creating a digital business, tackling the entire value chain at once. Companies getting this wrong often end up disappointed, abort the process, throw away what can be a substantial investment, and in the end, lose valuable time and watch competitors leap ahead. The potential of a promising new chapter becomes a setback.

However, giving your transformation team the task of assessing your value chain with care, identifying pain points and bottlenecks, particularly ones that squeeze cash flow, and singling out the right operation to liberate your business and executive thinking can propel your company on a path of previously unimagined growth and value creation.

This should not be guesswork. There is a data-driven, analytical approach that we will describe and illustrate. Fundamentally, your transformation team must first focus on portions of your operation where it is technologically feasible to transform them in a relatively short time frame, measured normally in weeks, not months, and making sure that whatever project you choose solves a critical problem that is directly linked to a top business priority, removing a pain point.

In that approach, the benefits will be obvious and compelling, energizing your employees and demonstrating the opportunities that await them and your leadership team. These are digital sprints, which are both challenging and empowering for your team. We will describe best practices that we have observed in numerous instances and, in many cases, that we have applied to deliver impressive results.

Zero In on Your Pain Points

Start with your value chain. Every company has one. This is the series of steps that starts with your suppliers and leads through the process of designing and producing your products or services and then proceeds to shipping and distribution to your customers and, ultimately, to consumers or end users. Begin with a granular, end-to-end image of the chain that identifies the inputs to your products, your company, and the products that you generate.

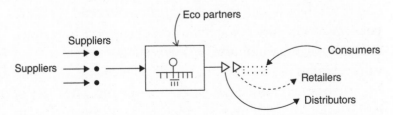

Then look at key money-making metrics across the chain. This will be an aid to guide the transformation team's discussions and planning. We find that it helps all team members visualize the business holistically so they can work together to single out opportunities as well as pain points. Where might there be cash leakage, redundancy, complexity, or waste? Those are areas where a digital platform could make a dramatic improvement in efficiencies and outcomes.

It's worth noting that most members of your team typically see this chain through a lens focused on their own business function. One purpose of developing this diagram in detail is to help them break free from that single-minded insularity. Your leaders need to see and register in their minds the entire flow from the beginning of the value chain to the end user and even to the post-sales consumer experience.

Once you have assembled and shared this tool, you should gather the transformation team members to start identifying the pain points—bottlenecks or dysfunctional processes—in all parts of the value chain and link them to cash flow and value creation where you can. For example, there could be too much inventory in the pipeline, a very common pain point that links directly to your cash. Or say you have excessive turnover in your call center. People are stressed, and customer data that could be useful to you is not being collected. That problem could translate into lower customer loyalty, more customer defections, reduced market share, and loss of revenue.

For example, in a pharmaceutical company, someone might observe, "You know, we have a high dropout rate of patients in our drug trials." A discussion of the issue with the group should emphasize all the implications of this problem. An excessively high dropout rate can lengthen the time required to transition from the discovery of a drug to its commercialization. That means expenses continue to mount, but revenues will kick in later than planned. Contrast that with the reality that commercializing a drug rapidly, without a drug trial slowdown, can accelerate the process of achieving a billion dollars in revenues. That should spotlight this pain point and underscore the clear benefits of resolving it.

For many companies, the most urgent pain points relate to cash deficiencies and cash traps. You need to analyze your value chain to clearly identify where cash flows may be getting stuck. Think through what is actually happening in your operations to cause the cash shortages. In some instances, erratic delivery schedules for supplies can cause problems.

If accounts receivable are swelling and holding up cash, look carefully at the causes. Why are customers not paying? Maybe your deliveries are late or unreliable. Amazon, for instance, confronted a last-mile delivery issue roughly a decade ago and had to make improvements to remove that particular pain point. Many other companies suffer from similar problems and often need help in accelerating cash flow.

Take Larsen & Toubro, a large construction company in India. They construct major infrastructure projects, such as power plants and institutional buildings, and they purchase about $6 billion in supplies a year in many different locations, a major logistical challenge. When a new CEO took over a few years ago, he decided the company needed to build a digital platform, a single source of truth, for this massive supply chain. He found it too decentralized, too expensive, with too much variation in delivery times. As a result, too much cash was trapped in the processes and inventories. There was also a pilferage problem.

The company hired a new executive to oversee the systems, and a group of digital enablers and data analytics experts were brought in. Looking at five years of supply chain data, they found the company was being hit with wide disparities in pricing, even from the same suppliers, lots of heavy indirect costs, such as energy costs for operating an inefficient system, and uneven delivery processes. Working with a digital enabler, the company was able to create a single source of truth to standardize, centralize, and analyze all information on the supply chain. Under the new digital business platform, the company saves about $600 million a year in its supply chain operations, enjoys greater reliability, and works with fewer suppliers.

Projectize Everything

You undoubtedly generated a long list of pain points, touching areas such as cash flow, suppliers, receivables, and customer satisfaction. Now you need to have your transformation team convert that list into a realistic set of bite-size project candidates. A retailer, for example, might explore what is preventing revenue growth and how building a digital platform and a single source of truth could gather and analyze the data needed to break through any bottlenecks. Is access to data and data analytics widely shared in the company? Do you need the capability to do dynamic pricing? Do you need faster new product innovation cycles? Would better on-time delivery systems help?

In your discussion, you are likely to discover that some of these pain points will have the same root cause and that, if carefully managed, one project could have multiple benefits. By projectizing your approach, you can apply management techniques that will focus on defining the deliverables, fixing the time frames for each "bite" in the process, establishing performance goals, and setting clear expectations that you can monitor and test as you proceed. You will find it easier to keep projects on track.

Ideally, a bite-size project, if well targeted, could deliver a turnkey outcome in 10 weeks or less. This is why including a technology specialist on your digital transformation team is critical. He or she can help judge whether each "bite," or issue, the team is trying to resolve is small enough to see a near-term benefit from digital intervention. Your technology team member may not have engaged in this exact process before but should have the experience and expertise needed to make a rough assessment, perhaps based on what they have learned from studying other companies.

Given the importance of ensuring you can deliver progress in that rough 10-week time frame, generating buy-in in your company and producing measurable results, you should make sure the boundaries of this first project are set so that it is achievable in the allotted time. The digital enabler you engage later will help verify and further refine the specifics. One way of gaining confidence is to devote a little more time to examining the digital process at other companies to learn from their experiences.

For example, at one alternative energy company the CEO recognized that a digital business could improve the efficiency of wind and solar power, so he invited people from consulting firms and nearby universities who had experience implementing digital technology to discuss and examine how they could be used. Then he called some noncompeting companies and asked to bring his management team to visit. The other companies were happy to host the team, some for half a day, where they presented a useful show-and-tell of their platform and its outcomes.

Among the most serious pain points you may discover as you examine your value chain are:

- Excessive inventories, which can tie up cash—so better balancing of supply and demand will free up cash;
- Inefficient internal processes and controls, which can bloat costs—so simplifying them can lower costs and increase margins;
- Static pricing models, which can hurt competitiveness—so developing dynamic pricing capabilities that respond in real-time can boost sales and market share; and
- Low customer loyalty, which raises costs and reduces revenues—so better use of data, feedback, and analytics can improve customer satisfaction and increase recurring revenues.

Reaching Deeper into Your Organization for Pain Point Insights

If you are particularly sensitive to gaining cultural acceptance for the digital transformation and generating positive social energy, here is another approach to identifying good project ideas and garnering support. One company we work with gathered a team of roughly 50 people and organized them into small groups, each of which was given four weeks to search for bite-size ideas for the projects. Another company, Indorama, embraced a similar process, organizing and then sending eight teams into the field for four weeks to do assessments. Inviting more people into the process invites broader buy-in.

A key advantage of this approach is that it includes people at lower organizational levels, who are closer to day-do-day interactions with suppliers or ecosystem partners, or in customer service and customer call centers. With their regular exposure to these routine interactions, they may spot pain points others operating at a more senior level would miss. The main benefit, though, is that these are the people who will be given much of the responsibility for implementing any digital solutions and making them succeed, and they should get lots of familiarity with the process and get acculturated to the new platform. Getting involved early may help overcome any fear or hesitancy they might have.

We have experienced numerous occasions when the fear of change is greater at higher organizational levels, where executives may feel overly attached to systems that got them to their current levels or are concerned about organizational disruptions that affect performance, while employees near the front lines are often eager to see the digital business and its single source of truth relieve the frustrations they may experience in their everyday work.

They see, often, that digital technology can be liberating. "What are we waiting for?" they often wonder. In those instances, the employees can become the advocates you need inside the organization and constant reminders that legacy approaches were just not working and needed to be replaced. Potentially, they become your digital ambassadors, helping build commitment among their peers, turning skeptics into believers.

Prioritize, Prioritize, Prioritize

With a list of bite-size projects in hand, the transformation team now has to prioritize them. You and your team must be aligned on the most promising and urgent projects, decisions that should take into account how long it will take each project "bite" to deliver a measurable outcome that links, in one way or another, to moneymaking. A quick financial return will build confidence and support across the team and the organization. And you won't have to go to the trouble of making the business case if the project will start earning a return in 10 weeks or less.

But the bite-size project you select should not only produce a quick return; it should have a visible impact on one of your company's top strategic priorities. The CEO, of course, knows what is most important to the business's success, whether related to revenues, costs, cash flow, customer satisfaction, brand visibility, or talent. Market cap may factor in heavily; a steady stream of revenue growth combined with lower costs is a formula for increasing market cap and value. The key is that value chain "bites" need to support these strategic goals, making the company's playbook more effective at creating value.

These first steps, establishing your priorities and deliverables, and sequencing them most effectively will require deep collaboration among your transformation team and the business's leadership, constant discussion, and balance between what is technologically doable and what propels your strategies forward.

Uncertain You Got It Right? Don't Hesitate to Restart

Maybe you have already started on a digital business journey. Determine where you are on a scale of "Not yet started" at one end to "Fully digital" at the other and how close you are to seeing payoffs from the project. This is a useful way to test your progress as well as whether you prioritized properly.

It is not rare for leaders to stop at this stage, reconsider whether they are really focused on the right steps to begin, and, if there is evidence you are not on the best track, back off and consider starting over. Keep in mind, the mark of an effective leader is not trudging forward on a plan no matter what but to be willing to constantly test plans, assess effectiveness, and course correct as needed.

There is nothing wrong with restarting; in fact, if you are on a path that does not support your strategic goals or that will not achieve measurable results in a reasonable period of time, it is better to pause and think carefully about how to get it right. We know from research that some 90 percent of transformation initiatives either tread water and begin failing or have been abandoned. These difficulties cost you time, discourage leadership and employees, and allow the company to lose ground to the competition. It is smart to adjust as needed, but you cannot completely give up on the idea of digitalization.

We recommend you go through the mental exercises this chapter outlines to be sure your projects are small enough to complete in a very short time horizon and that your priorities are correct for your business. Carefully evaluate the process for identifying pain points and defining your projects, and then test your choices against your strategic priorities.

It is better, if necessary, to swallow the sunk costs and redefine your path if that is the price of getting it right and reenergizing your transformation team.

A major retailer we worked with reached this juncture after considerable investment in a project designed to streamline its supply chain. After it paused to take stock, the company found it was suffering from a lack of tangible progress, which meant that inefficiencies persisted or even worsened. The CEO reluctantly pulled the plug. He noted that one part of the problem was how the company had defined the issue, the pain point, it wanted to fix. Another problem was the digital enabler's inability to deliver a simple solution. The best course of action, the CEO decided, was to start over.

Any rethinking and restarting of your transformation should include a focus on internal actions at your company as well as external steps to coordinate with your digital enabler and understand your markets. Remember, your digital partner must be your key collaborator cutting through complexity to get the right data to the right people at the right time and building analytics capabilities that turn data into reusable assets. That is your North Star. Follow it faithfully!

That is why the next step in the process is selecting the right digital enabler for you and building the right working relationship.

5

Launch!

You are on the cusp of your digital transformation. You have selected and empowered your transformation team, articulated your priorities, and agreed on the pain point that will be the first "bite" you attack. Your leadership teams are on board and fully synchronized.

You are ready to press the accelerator pedal. The digital enabler will be an indispensable strategic partner and a catalyst for making innovation and collaboration the air the members of your business breathe. This is how you begin.

Finding Digital Enablers

An entire cottage industry has emerged of digital enablers that possess a golden toolbox—including software engineering expertise, skill in developing and deploying algorithms and AI enhancements, and experience in assembling comprehensive digital platforms that will revolutionize your business opportunities, value creation, and executive decision making. These practitioners can assess your company and its needs, prepare the bite-size phases and sequencing, build turnkey systems, and teach your staff how to benefit from their advantages. But where to start?

Step one, build your list of candidates. This can require some care, since you can't open the Yellow Pages to "digital enablers" and identify options. Firms often identify themselves differently and may be well known to IT experts but have a lower profile outside the field. A small amount of effort, though, will pay off. Move swiftly.

- Turning to your IT department is one good place to begin.
- Business consultants you already work with may have suggestions.
- You should check if your competitors have worked with digital enablers.
- You can go to a search engine and type in, "digital transformation solution companies."
- Read through the explanations these companies provide of how they work and what they have achieved.

What is critical is that you remember you are hiring a partner and strategic collaborator who will be your guide and business solutions supporter for a long time. You are not outsourcing the transformation! The digital enabler is not a coding and software specialist who comes in, gets a list of specifications, and then, months later, hands you a final digital package. You are seeking a deeper form of compatibility, where the focus is always on your business and its needs and a productive dialogue.

Altimetrik, which Raj owns and runs, is one such digital enabler. Some other highly capable firms we have experience with include UST Global, Fractal Analytics, and Egen, which have done many bite-size digital projects at different types of companies in different business sectors.

Many in-house IT departments believe they have the capability to drive the transformation themselves, but in our experience they often lack deep expertise with algorithms, data analytics, and AI applications and an ability to seamlessly meld all these capabilities in a user-friendly platform. Even an excellent department is usually not equipped to navigate this journey end-to-end with the right degree of sophistication. A smart vendor will bring an outsider's unique perspective, as well as an outsider's insights, and, perhaps most important, experience with many other companies and the practical strategies that come from repeated hands-on encounters.

Remember, the goal is to move the needle for your business and its moneymaking capabilities, not just for your technology. Make this your leadership team's daily mantra!

An approach some companies, particularly bigger corporations, are attracted to is the so-called big-bang project, which tackles your entire value chain, end-to-end and all at once. It is conceived of as one massive project that is handed over to one of the larger consulting firms, such as Accenture or McKinsey, and handed back when completed. These firms have a great deal of expertise, of course, and one of the factors that can influence this decision is how active a role the company's CEO wants to play, along with the leadership team, in the process.

In our experience, this approach carries risks that you need to bear in mind. The first is time. From the launch to the conclusion, a big-bang approach can take as long as two years. In the accelerated pace of change in our knowledge economy, the technology and software may be obsolete by the time the project is finished or the market may have passed you by. Also, some of these large consulting firms subcontract out portions of the work to smaller digital enablers with their unique expertise. Why put a middleman between your transformation team and the digital enabler?

Another risk is that, if the project is undertaken without constant, direct collaboration, you may not know if the new platform actually responds to your strategic priorities until it is too late to adjust the process to fit the objectives.

And last, whether this type of approach to building a digital business will actually produce the business and moneymaking outcomes you require is uncertain and may take too long.

That is why we have tried to demystify our digital business roadmap so you will understand why a bite-size, sequential approach can produce much faster performance improvements—in weeks or months, not years—balanced social and structural changes in your organization through a collaborative process, long-term support from the digital enabler as you change and grow, and better buy-in from your team. And, importantly, at far less cost.

Our model provides a new paradigm for addressing digital businesses and building a new growth trajectory. Embrace the possibilities!

Selecting Your Digital Enabler

When it comes to choosing a vendor from the final list, you may feel some trepidation about the best method for asking the right questions and comparing the firms on a consistent basis. You overcome that with a structured interviewing process that is consistent and transparent to everyone on your team.

It helps to use a template during your interviews and the evaluation process. This will ensure you ask each candidate the right questions and have a common basis for comparing once you are narrowing down your search. Usually, interviews can take from one to two hours each, so you need to be focused.

Among the criteria you should employ:

- Check to make sure they have the financial capacity to see your project through without interference from their other obligations.
- Ask many questions about their technological capacity and familiarity with different types of tools, software, and platforms.
- Does the vendor articulate an understanding of your pain points and talk about business outcomes rather than technological specifications? Have they worked in your industry previously?
- Does the vendor talk in terms of providing a user-friendly platform with excellent visualization, a dashboard, a single source of truth, and data standardization, even if data comes from many different sources?

- Do they talk about simplifying and streamlining data flows and applying AI and algorithms to deliver actionable insights that can become reusable assets?
- Are they good listeners, understanding your challenges quickly, and do you feel you make a strong personal connection that will enhance your collaboration?
- Will they be strategic partners who can work closely with your company's talent to help them internalize a culture of collaboration between businesspeople and technology teams?
- Do they talk like a partner and invite a partnership approach to the process? Do they regard the relationship as ongoing to assist in your company's evolution or as a one-off project?
- Pricing, of course, is a significant issue. How do they charge? Some vendors have a subscription, cloud-based model, which means much smaller up-front costs and easy updates to the software as needed. These month-by-month costs extend payments and maintain the vendor relationship.

Remember, again, that you should not place too heavy an emphasis on finding a vendor who creates all your software from scratch. Commonly, some of the tools your vendor will deploy are off-the-shelf rather than custom designed. We have found that 80 to 90 percent of the software tools, the algorithms, and platform elements can be off-the-shelf products. This is often a strength rather than a shortcoming.

That, for instance, was the case with the retailer that needed a crash program to build its e-commerce site when the pandemic shutdown hit early in 2020. As they partnered with the digital enabler UST Global, the new platform was assembled quickly using some off-the-shelf programs that were customized in how they connected and functioned with the company's systems and supply chains, delivering exceptional new opportunities for the clothing retailer and its customers.

And bear in mind that most vendors have a great deal of practice giving their initial pitches, and so they generally perform well. So you must look beneath the polished surface. The question you must address is whether they understand your pain points and your business strategy, whether they have resolved these issues in previous engagements, and whether they understand that the technology is just a facilitator on the path to improved business outcomes.

Look at how each practitioner describes their approach. Are they solution merchants or collaborators? Do they provide case studies of their clients and list those clients as potential references? Do they describe themselves as producers of discrete technology packages or as partners in an ongoing process? Do they accentuate the complexity or simplicity of their solutions?

In our experience, the more code that the engineers produce, the more problems that are likely to pop up. So find a vendor that takes a product approach, meaning they are focused on the best outcomes for your business rather than technological brainteasers. They must provide solutions whose simplicity and effectiveness they can describe in plain language and that your business team can easily visualize and utilize effectively.

The CEO of Coca-Cola HBC, the Swiss-based Coca-Cola bottler mentioned in Chapter 2, came to me (Ram) several years ago with a number of problems relating to the data senior executives were receiving on markets and product performance. Coca-Cola HBC covers a lot of territories—it operates in 28 countries, from Ireland to Eastern Russia and then south to Nigeria—and having trusted information in a standardized format is essential to developing priorities for budgeting, new product introductions, expansion, or pullbacks. But the CEO, Zoran Bogdanovic, was frustrated by information systems that were walled off in silos and, in some instances, protected by turf-conscious executives. This led to skepticism about the trustworthiness of the data and created tensions among senior executives.

I explained that Zoran and his leadership teams needed a single source of truth, a transparent digital system on a platform that would collect and standardize data and then apply algorithms and AI to develop actionable insights, market projections, and other reusable assets along with consensus about priorities and initiatives.

I moved quickly, discussing digital enablers that I was familiar with, with input from their CTO, and ended up with three candidates, including UST Global, a software firm I knew well and had worked with before, and Fractal Analytics, a digital enabler that had previously worked with a major Coca-Cola bottler in the US.

We invited each firm to give us presentations following a strict format. We provided a detailed set of specifications and instructions on the objectives, creation of a single source of truth, and a dashboard for monitoring performance and asked that each firm describe the platform they would design.

Each firm was given a strict limit of 40 minutes for the presentation, to be followed by an hour and twenty minutes of discussion. The meetings were held at Coca-Cola HBC's offices in Zurich, all on the same day. Each team could bring a maximum of three people, but they could include others on videoconferencing if they wanted.

The presentations went briskly, and Fractal Analytics demonstrated its strong understanding of the bottling business. One unexpected twist came in the UST Global presentation. They had looked into and discussed some issues involving the enterprise resource planning software, from SAP, that Coca-Cola HBC used and its compatibility with a new data platform. They suggested some additional work might be required to make certain that the systems melded seamlessly and produced the best data analytics.

We created a sort of flipchart summary for each firm for easy visualization and comparison and made a decision later the same day. The company retained Fractal Analytics for the overall job and UST Global to work on the SAP compatibility issue.

We had been open minded in our analysis of the candidates and learned something new. That is the approach you should take.

Structuring Your Partnership

Once you have selected your digital enabler, begin by defining what success looks like.

This first act of engagement is where your practitioner at the digital enabler can help you cut through to the root cause of your challenges and how you can resolve them.

Typically, this initial discussion will include provision for development of the single source of truth, a dashboard for visualization of your data and value chain mechanics. It should be made clear how these tools will support and accelerate decision making.

Take, for example, the maker of luxury candies based in Europe. Its products are delicious but surprisingly complex. The chocolates are not standardized; they are different sizes and shapes, and ingredients vary. The chocolates have a limited shelf life. That requires complex supply chains that must be integrated and operated in tandem on tight time schedules.

But some time ago the company was running into problems of coordination in some parts of the production and packaging processes. That was painfully evident, for example, when it produced a large number of boxes of chocolates for a customer but did not have an inventory of the distinctive labels that are attached to the boxes. The supply chain was disordered, affecting deliveries.

Altimetrik was hired as their digital enabler, and it quickly found that the candy maker did not have a centralized global inventory system—a single source of truth—nor did it have a centralized ordering system or a means for visualizing that system and coordinating all the strands.

Altimetrik identified the problem as not simply one of technology—the company relied on old mainframe computers, which were adequate—but of integration of all the information flows for the materials involved in manufacturing the candies and the timing of deliveries.

They had to develop a system to streamline and unify all the ordering processes, build a single source of truth that provided a comprehensive overview of the supply chain and inventories, and a process for delivering real-time alerts when bottlenecks or shortages occurred. The changes created a new end-to-end, coordinated system and then deployed AI and ML to develop projections (reusable assets) based on historical patterns to assist in inventory management.

In another example, a fintech company that connects investors eager to make loans with small businesses seeking loans was having difficulty with its risk analytics and asked Altimetrik to work on digital solutions. Altimetrik simplified the problem by capturing more data from the web on the borrowers, markets, and overall economic conditions and applying digital analytics to organize that information. It put this data platform into the cloud, smoothed out the systems for capturing critical financial data on borrowers, and introduced algorithms, machine learning, and powerful analytics to better assess the risks associated with the loans.

As a result, the fintech company had access to more up-to-date data for its risk assessments and more up-to-date risk models. Previously, it had taken the company from seven to eight months to refresh the risk assessment models using the most contemporary data. In the new platform, refreshing the models can be done in four to six weeks. In addition, with the system moved to the cloud, it follows a pay-as-you-go model, which spreads out the costs to the fintech company.

In establishing the roadmap with the digital enabler, the discussion should include the KPIs you will employ for measuring success and identifying deviations quickly. These KPIs should be agreed on with your digital practitioners so there is transparency about progress and agreement on how you will address problems or new information.

Your initial discussion should also include construction of a list of all the key stakeholders and their roles in aligning the project with its goals. As part of this process, expectations should be established for the frequency of updates and other communications.

This is an iterative process, not just presentation of a plan that will then be pursued until completion. You must build into your work a feedback loop so that the CEO and the transformation team can respond to the progress, bugs that emerge, or new ideas that may arise as the team observes the digital platform and single source of truth in action. Objectives can and in many cases should evolve as the digital engineers learn more about your business and you learn more about the power of the new tools, the algorithms, and data analytics. You will take a product approach with engineering discipline, creating an engineering environment to translate insights and ideas into marketable products.

Briefing your CEO regularly can be critical to the success of the effort. The direct participation of the CEO, who should be visible, sends a message to the whole company and all stakeholders that this is a high priority and that everyone needs to fall in line. It demonstrates CEO commitment and supports deep engagement and buy-in.

Of course, there are always ways a project, even one that is well planned, can get off track. Numerous issues can emerge in the nitty-gritty of the process that can cause trouble. The CEO or czar should watch for these and address them right away.

Here are some typical examples:

- Your IT department may have its own pet digital projects and attempt to subtly shift the digital enabler toward those goals rather than the bigger strategic objectives for the business.
- Because of security protocols or internal resistance to the changes in the business, the digital enabler may be denied access to critical information or systems. Those barriers must be removed.
- As a dialogue develops with your business departments and they convey challenges or problems they may be facing, the project might morph in an unintended direction. Close, persistent monitoring can keep it on track.

Once each bite-size piece of your value chain is transformed and the pain point issues addressed, you need to discuss a longer-range governance plan that will include having your business teams take ownership of the platform and single source of truth and embrace a process of continuous growth and evolution. This is integral to your transformation and should continue the collaboration with your digital enabler.

A good example of this follow-up process was how Altimetrik tackled a problem at a major bank. They had a successful electronic money transfer business involving mostly large transactions between commercial entities. But some years ago the introduction of a number of apps made such transfers accessible to consumers, who often moved far smaller sums of money. This became a high-volume business involving much smaller individual transfers.

The bank wanted to preserve its legacy money transfer business but also create a new platform that would allow it to build a presence in the consumer-oriented business. It hired Altimetrik to help develop a new digital platform. Altimetrik developed a system of separate domains to house and protect the legacy business so it would not be disrupted as the new platform was constructed.

Altimetrik worked closely with the bank to ensure that key personnel took ownership of the new platform and help it evolve new capabilities as needed. Altimetrik provided agility coaches to train bank officials in the use of the system and to adjust the bank's culture to take full advantage of the capabilities of the platform. In other words, Altimetrik helped make certain that this was not just a technological solution to a business problem but a new business opportunity.

This is a journey you have just begun, but you will continue for a long time. Where will you take this transformation?

6

From Algorithms to New Models

Creating Stepped-Up Value for Customers and Shareholders

You have taken the first "bite" in your value chain, and you now have a new platform and new capabilities. You are developing reusable assets and benefiting from the single source of truth. You're already seeing performance benefits. You have eliminated a pain point, implemented a new algorithmic digital engine, and incentivized your managers. Your people are on board. Relationships within your business are more collaborative and dynamic, and innovation is bubbling up from an energized workforce.

You are now in possession of a powerful and agile value multiplier—both the technology side of this equation and the people side. This is when senior management should step back and reimagine your business strategy and new sources of competitive advantage. You are becoming vastly more adept at serving customers and your shareholders and accelerating moneymaking.

This is where vision meets results. What's next?

Specifically, you're ready for the second "bite" of the value chain, but it is with a new perspective. Your managers are not just ready to continue this sequential process, they are eager, having experienced the initial success. Because your leadership team is now familiar with the process, they will feel less threatened by the technology and better at understanding how it can help them do their work, make decisions faster, and empower staff. With each new digital bite, the impact on your performance will be amplified.

What you will soon realize is the prismatic character of these advances. Processes and methods that used to be one-sided and linear are now multidimensional and capable of delivering nonlinear increases in cash flow and value.

A good example is the establishment of new direct, online channels to consumers. Sales will rise, but—even more important—you will realize a significant increase in data about your customers and the markets. AI and ML will help translate that flow into deep insights, into those valuable reusable assets, which will inform your marketing strategies, your new product development, and push into new markets. Your customers, much better served, will increase their engagement, increasing the data flow and further enhancing your capability for navigating valuable new markets.

Walmart, once a digital laggard, eventually did it, increasing its market capitalization from less than $200 billion in 2015 to $400 billion today. Adobe did it, propelling a rocket-like rise in its market capitalization to $289 billion from $45 billion at the end of 2015. Disney did it, moving aggressively into streaming and adding to its content creation capabilities, sending its market cap to $325 billion from $173 billion in 2015.

Those large companies recognized and have taken advantage of the benefits of building the digital business. They may be lagging digital giants such as Amazon and Netflix—just two examples—but they now possess that power and are using it to catch up quickly. Small and mid-sized companies now have our model to achieve these game-changing benefits—quickly and inexpensively. That can open the floodgates of opportunity. Combined with creative thinking and execution, you can place yourself on a path of exponential growth.

As you push forward on this path and proceed sequentially, tackling your value chain one piece at a time, here are five key areas where you can use this new leverage to accelerate performance:

- Focus on the consumer. Companies now need to be adaptable and consumer-obsessed for warp-speed growth and faster cash generation.
- Be sure you have the right kind of talent to spot and pursue new opportunities and to operate in the more open, flatter, collaborative work culture you are creating. Turn the old dogma about people on its head: actively bring disruptors—meaning people who innovate and question the status quo—into your company. Seek a new breed of leader who understands and embraces these disruptors, the soul of innovation.
- Redesign the decision-making process to speed it up and increase transparency. Reduce the number of

people who review the issues and the committees that routinely used to be involved in consultation. Bring in the operators, the people who have their feet on the ground and understand the real impact of every decision on your customers. Open up operating mechanisms and expand the rewards for original initiatives.

- Search for other ways to use this dynamic new flow of data, your single source of truth, with your digital platform, including dashboards and clear visualization. Provide training across the board so people can make use of the analytics.

- Ensure your leadership is in tune with the culture changes that come with greater transparency. This depoliticizes and de-bureaucratizes the workplace. Keep in mind that your employees already have an enhanced appreciation and understanding of digital businesses due to the Covid-19 shutdown. This makes your job easier.

This is a rare opportunity not just to reorganize your company and articulate new strategic priorities but to embrace changes that will help you see your markets and operate more like a digital native. The process will feed on itself and turbocharge your advances as long as you are taking time to ensure you have the right kind of leadership talent in place and the improved decision-making model.

Your company's talent must understand, observe, and constantly be analyzing consumer behavior, using algorithms and AI to identify important shifts in spending or desires. You and your leaders must embrace a rule that innovation is not negotiable. The talent must be focused on experimentation and they must tolerate occasional failures and see them as learning opportunities. These are a means of generating revenue productivity, a strategic must.

And do not lose sight of the fact that nothing stands still in your new digital business world. Today's new idea, even tomorrow's innovation, will face obsolescence sooner than you may expect. Do not regard that reality as harmful. See it as an opportunity to deploy your new platform to push further ahead of your competitors and to enhance your broader vision of competitive advantage, an iterative process.

It is in the DNA of your AI tools that they learn with each new piece of data. They get "smarter," and they give you increasingly valuable insights into how to serve your customers. That is why your reusable assets always become more valuable. But to fully take advantage of those tools and insights never cut back on training for your talent. You need to build a steady diet of training and learning into your corporate routine.

Rethinking your decision-making processes must also be core elements of your adjusted operating methods. Changing the flow of data—making it more open and subject to analytics tools—should translate into fewer and faster decisions. AI will make many routine decisions for you. Often, these decisions will be pushed down several levels, where teams will be collaborating on the front lines of customer engagement.

Eliminating the number of steps in operations and decision making will also contribute to the reorganization working its way through your structure. You will need fewer middle managers, but they will be more productive. They will find their jobs more stimulating, enriching, as they devote less time to direct oversight and more on enhancing business performance. Their oversight commitments, in fact, will go down to close to zero. Instead, the amount of management coaching will increase, placing most of your managers on the cutting edge of the data analytics.

The new breed of leader will possess real expertise and be respected by subordinates both for this deep knowledge as well as their ability to motivate and support their teams. They will be respected for the quality of their insights and foresight.

You are now at the moment when you will write the next chapter in your company's growth. You have mastered this innovative model for reimagining the business. The tools give you a new kind of 360 vision, allowing you to see farther, in more detail and depth. You will identify numerous opportunities for nonlinear growth, and you will understand your customers as never before. Your digital future is not tomorrow, it's today.

7

What Can Go Wrong and How to Make It Right

Rising to the Leadership Challenge

Even bite-size projects can be stalled, and there are lessons to be learned from companies that have hit some snags. The most important of these is for the CEO (or digital surrogate) to stay deeply engaged throughout. You will find no substitutes for learning and paying attention to how well the execution is progressing.

This is by no means a passive role. The point of that engagement is to do a quick diagnosis at the first hint of a problem and to be decisive in executing a remedy. Unless top leaders use their full toolkit—including actions like reallocating resources, changing people, and coaching on behavior—they themselves can become the roadblock. You can learn as much from other leaders' missteps as you can from their success.

Reckoning with a Bad Hire

A common problem that can be ruinous for even a bite-size approach is recruiting the wrong chief digital officer. It is an easy mistake to make given that the executives who do the hiring usually know little about digitization and use of AI and so on. Our observation and experience across the globe is that while the batting average for new hires is not perfect, for CDOs it is much worse. CEOs have to own up to having made a wrong decision and move quickly to fix it, because the longer they wait, the larger the resulting competitive disadvantage for their companies.

A mistake in this critical hire is what slowed the digitalization of a large high-performing manufacturing company. Based in Malaysia, it had built itself into a global powerhouse with some $5 billion in revenues by acquiring manufacturers around the world over several decades. It had operations on multiple continents, in countries including China, the US, Indonesia, Germany, and Brazil. Only a small percentage of its revenue came from its home country.

Almost all the company's global revenue was in hard currency, and it had the normal issues of global politics, the US–China economic war, and the volatility of funds flowing from one country to another. When the Covid-19 pandemic hit, the company sometimes had to shut down facilities on short notice, which interrupted the supply chain. Because of volatility in both demand and the supply chain, forecasting was extremely difficult. Volatility could be as much as 100 percent, which is like seeing the price of oil jumping from $40 to $80 and then back down to $40.

The company managed all of those things well considering they were done manually or on spreadsheets, but its clunky forecasting was becoming increasingly problematic and putting the company at a competitive disadvantage. Digitalization had become a necessity. Yet the growth-by-acquisition strategy made it difficult because each acquisition had brought with it a different IT system, some of which were becoming obsolete. Getting all of them to work together would require a lot of capital investment and consume a lot of cash in what was already a capital-intensive business.

As the CEO was preparing to take the plunge into digitalization, he got news that increased his sense of urgency. He learned from one of his advisors that Amazon had entered into logistics in his company's industry. He had seen that when Amazon digitalized its logistics from delivery station to the customer, it cut costs by a factor of 4 and reduced the cycle time to the customer by a factor of 2 and also reduced inventory, freed up cash, and strengthened customer relationships. He immediately knew that the digital giant's incursion could profoundly affect his business.

The CEO turned to a long-time senior executive to oversee the company's digitalization efforts along with continuing to run building products, and the senior executive soon put together a two-year program to fix the disparate IT systems as the crucial first step. Then came the question about whether to hire a digital officer from outside to lead the initiative, and if so, what the specifics should be.

It was decided that the heads of HR and strategy would work with a headhunting firm to find the right outside candidate to be the new chief digital officer. After interviewing several people, the two executives chose a 35-year-old who had worked at a number of highly respected large companies in Europe and Asia.

The new CDO spent his first five months traveling the globe to visit the company's various locations. He talked to more than 90 people from across the company to learn what was needed and how they were currently doing things and to understand more about the company in general. Then he spent some time putting together a 75-page report that he would present to the CEO, the senior executive who had outlined a two-year program to fix IT, and a handful of other C-suite executives.

As the CEO listened intently to the CDO, he became very uneasy. "It was as if he were building the Taj Mahal," the CEO later told us. "He said he would need to recruit 91 people to build it, but there was no discussion of how it would be done, there were no specifics about what interim projects or steps would be taken, or how exactly he would proceed."

The CEO couldn't help but wonder, Had this young CDO ever implemented anything anywhere that even approached the complexity of meshing these fragmented systems and data? His resume had an impressive list of companies, but the CEO recalled that he had switched jobs roughly every two and a half years. Did he ever drive a project to completion and scale it up?

The CEO wanted to check, so he asked one of his advisors to reach out to the chief executive of the company where the CDO had most recently worked. Yes, the CDO had in fact worked there, for just two years and four months. No, he had not done anything particularly significant, and there was no record of him having implemented any project.

Now what? The CEO had grave misgivings that the CDO could handle the job they hired him to do, and there was no room for failure. Should they test him on a smaller project? Should they immediately hire someone else? The options were not appealing, but the CEO decided to give the CDO a smaller project and find a more experienced person to lead the bigger digitalization initiative.

The new search launched with revised specifications for the job, new headhunters, and this time around, the CEO's participation in the interviews. The CEO had come to see the benefit of spending his personal time to probe the candidates.

Recruiting proved difficult, however. Nobody wanted to move to company headquarters in Malaysia because of the country's small size and political turmoil. What broke the standstill was the CEO's timely decision to create a digitalization office elsewhere, in a Western country where top technologists like to live and work. Finally the company could get on track, but the wrong hire had meanwhile delayed the company's efforts by one year and allowed the competition to gain ground.

An Organizational Impasse Unaddressed

The CEO of Torgate Inc. (all names are disguised) had all but given up on having his son, Mike, join the family business. But after spending 20 years in consulting and management following his MBA, Mike stepped in to lead Torgate's innovation and technology group. He reported to Ross, the company's president and likely successor to Mike's dad, who was getting ready to retire.

The company has two divisions, one is chemicals, the other is building products, with no real connection between the two. Building products was run by Harry, a highly regarded company veteran. Everyone knew that if they wanted something done, call Harry. He had great interpersonal skills, was trusted, and knew how to navigate through the organization to get to the right information or the right person. He had originally joined the company on the chemical side but had made an excellent adaptation to run building products.

Building products is a fragmented industry, meaning that there are many suppliers who sell to small companies as well as big enterprises such as Home Depot and Lowe's. Harry helped grow the division through acquisitions of smaller businesses, some with proprietary materials or proprietary manufacturing systems. He also kept operations sharp with people who were highly professional and successful.

The two business divisions have striking differences. In building products, product is the name of the game, so the company strives to lead with innovative products. It also tries to run its manufacturing and logistics very efficiently. The multibillion-dollar chemical business, on the other hand, is basically a commodity business. It is highly volatile because its pricing depends on crude oil prices, which are determined by the commodities market.

Mike had a technology background and wanted to help prepare the company to digitalize. He brought in an advisor who, among other things, took Mike, Ross, and Harry on tours of companies that had made good progress on digitalization. Everyone, including the CEO and the board, was eager to get out of the gate. They enthusiastically hired Dimitri, a leader with digitalization in his background, to lead the effort, and had him report to Harry.

Dimitri recruited a few experts who could clean up data from different systems and had expertise in AI and machine learning, and took some time to do benchmarking where digitization was going on, and to interview people in the organization. About four months in, he scheduled a workshop for both divisions of the company combined. That idea met some resistance, not from lower-level employees but from Harry and Mike, two of the executives who were most deeply involved in digitization to date and had been instrumental in hiring Dimitri. They thought Dimitri needed to first learn about the small projects the building products division already had underway.

Dimitri postponed the workshop and instead laid out a detailed plan for digitizing both parts of the company, which included creating a single source of truth for the whole company. He showed what the projects and priorities should be and for each project, defined in parentheses who would be the outsourcing partners. It was an impressive list, and Dimitri showed great skill in presenting it. He made a strong case to line up business sponsors for each project, do the sequencing, and get going.

As Mike saw it, there was one glaring problem: it wasn't Dimitri's work. Someone who had since left the company had prepared what Dimitri presented as his own. On top of that, the idea of creating a single source of truth for the whole company didn't make sense given how different the businesses were. There could be no benefit from economies of scale because customer data could in no way be synthesized.

Seven months after recruiting their CDO, the company was at a standstill, debating whether they should have two digitization efforts or one, two CDOs or one, and whether Dimitri should stay in the job. It was time for the CEO to step in, overcome the indecision, and get the two divisions on a fast track to digitalize.

Smooth Sailing with the CEO's Engagement

Successful initiatives have a common thread: the top leader stays deeply involved throughout. One obvious benefit is signaling that the project is important, but there's more. It means the CEO can provide coaching when behavior needs to change, get a conflict resolved, or make a fast decision on human or financial resources to keep things moving at pace.

One CEO stands out in our minds as exemplifying the kind of learning and engagement that makes digital projects go smoothly and have the desired impact. He is the head of an 11-year-old Indian company that provides alternative energy via wind and solar power. This is a very capital-intensive business, so the company has to borrow lots of money to fund the installment of solar panels and wind turbines. To sell the energy it generates, the company bids for contracts with the Indian government. These contracts are long term; they specify a fixed price that the company cannot exceed for 25 years.

The state governments in India are responsible for the distribution of electricity that passes through to them, and most use state-owned power distribution companies for that. What poses challenges for an energy-producing company is that state governments in India are notorious for not paying bills. Every time the government changes from one political party to another, the payments are delayed. Accounts receivable have been known to stretch to one year. Such delays put a huge strain on cash, making it hard for the company to make payments on the money it borrows for its huge capital investments, and also increases its need for working capital.

The company's highest cost is interest on its borrowing. Labor is a very small part of its expenses.

In the past few years, bidding on contracts has become more competitive, and prices on long-term contracts declined by 20 percent. Digitalization came to be an important element in making the company's moneymaking model succeed in the face of those market challenges.

The CEO had no specific knowledge of technology, but he was and is a voracious reader. He was well aware that some companies had done amazing things by digitalizing their businesses, and those stories sparked his curiosity. "In the beginning it was a nebulous idea," he told us. "I didn't have a clear picture of what it could do for our business. But I believed it was the next big thing and would create a lot of value, and I wanted to learn how it could translate to our specific context."

Being one of those people who is naturally curious, the CEO was determined to learn more and to take his team on the learning journey with him. They spent about a year speaking to potential vendors who operated in the space and to other companies internationally. The CEO arranged for tutors and people who had digitalized their company to come to the office and share their experiences with the team. He gathered a number of case studies to work through.

The board was looped into the learning as well. The CEO had a good relationship with them and kept communication open as he and his team visited companies in other industries where digital technology had been successfully implemented. Those companies included Larsen & Toubro, renowned for its early and transformative digitalization, and a range of manufacturers in India, Europe, and the US. The CEO and team were especially keen to explore the problems companies had when implementing their plans, information they subsequently shared with the board.

After this period of real-world research, the CEO and his team were mentally prepared to start their digitalization journey. They determined that the necessary first step was to gather data and put it in a meaningful, analyzable form. For that, they used consulting firm McKinsey & Company, which made the data usable and also showed the team the kinds of exciting things they could do with it.

Most of the opportunities to make an impact on the business were not off-the-shelf applications, a fact that prompted the CEO to seek a small digital enabler to partner with. The CEO took an active role in quickly selecting one and working closely with them to get their best thinking about how to improve the efficiency of the wind turbines and solar panels. The CEO also convinced the small digital vendor to carry the project to completion while he himself, along with his chief operating officer, would supervise it so they would be able to maximize their learning.

The CEO did in fact continue to work directly with the digital enabler, which completed a small project that delivered results in nine months. His close contact gave him an idea: Why not acquire the digital enabler, thereby bringing the expertise in-house? The team that had done the benchmarking of other companies' digitalization efforts agreed, and the details of the acquisition were worked out.

Within a year, the deal was done, and two new digital projects were completed with the CEO's ongoing involvement. The new projects increased the efficiency of solar and wind power generation and made it possible for management to track multiple metrics and slice the data in various ways, such as by time of day. They produced an annual savings of $2 million, which would go toward the cost of the acquisition.

Project completion was not the end goal. Making the company more competitive is, and those efforts are ongoing. The company now has a full-fledged digital unit focused on continuously innovating around the use of data and algorithms. Prices cannot be changed, but efficiency can be and how power is stored can be. It is now possible to create new energy products that are priced at a premium for a new market segment. Also, the company now has more confidence when bidding for government contracts it will be locked into long term.

As new follow-on projects get designed, the organization supports them. The smooth adoption and positive outcomes of digital projects are in no small measure attributable to a CEO who took an interest, did the work of learning from others, and by staying engaged throughout the process, brought his team members, board, and

the organization to where they drive—not impede—
the changes.

At a time when people were content to manage assets
as they always had, the CEO pushed them to try something new, despite the fact that his own thinking about
digitalization was still nebulous. When McKinsey painted
a picture of the kinds of things the company could do, the
CEO made sure that the whole team was exposed to relevant information so they would share the excitement.
He committed the resources to bring necessary expertise
in-house, and reassigned people to leverage the newly
acquired capability as a business asset. These and other
actions demonstrate how specific acts of leadership can
create real business benefits.

Part Two

8

Low Investment, High Impact Digital Business Themes: Use Cases

1. Innovative Blockchain Solution for a Mid-sized Agribusiness Company 83
2. Cloud-Native Banking Platform for Gig Workers 85
3. Digital Decisioning Platform for Global Confectionary Producer 88
4. Payment Platform to Securely Scan and Classify Data 93
5. Identity as a Service: Connecting Customers for Better Targeting 98
6. Payment Platform Modernization for Large US Bank 101
7. Improving Profit Margin and Cash Flow for Small Businesses with Instant Payment 105
8. Consumer Lending Platform for Mid-tier US Banks 107

9. Physician Directory 110

10. Virtual Product Development Platform 112

11. Modern Expense Management for Commercial Cards 114

12. Demand Forecasting and Logistics Optimization for CPG/FMCG 116

13. Targeted Marketing Campaign for P2P Lenders 119

14. Single Source of Truth – Connected Sales, Revenue, and Demand Planning 121

15. Situational Awareness 123

16. Remote Patient Management Services for Critical Illness 125

17. Mobile Apps for SMBs in Health-Care Network 128

18. Incorporating Voice of Customer to Improve Customer Satisfaction 130

19. Conversational Artificial Intelligence Platform 132

20. Process Warehouse Automation 134

21. Open Account Trade 136

22. Fleet Management through Artificial Intelligence–Based Simulation 138

23. Digital Shopping Experience for Home Décor through Augmented Reality 140

24. Digital Marketing-Driven Sales at Institutional Fund Managers 142

25. Payment Network Interchange Fees Revenue Leakage 145

26. Rapid Medi-Claim Authorization Platform 147

1. Innovative Blockchain Solution for a Mid-sized Agribusiness Company

Pain Points

This company is in the business of large-scale production of vegetables in greenhouses. The decision makers in the company had heard of Walmart and other larger players implementing blockchain for some of their supply chains. The questions in front of this company were, "While it makes sense for larger buyers to implement a blockchain driven supply chain, does it make sense for relatively smaller companies like us? If yes, how can we leverage the strength of this emerging paradigm called blockchain?"

They hired a digital business partner to put an appropriate solution in place.

The digital business partner applied the principles of simplification, innovation, and a single source of truth to address the above concerns.

Solution Approach The typical industry implementation of blockchain requires buy-in from several companies. This, by itself, makes the whole implementation process too complex and time consuming. To simplify the process, the digital business vendor proposed that the agribusiness company pick a smaller use case with fewer "hops" (number of companies involved in the chain).

Next, the vendor suggested that the company break away from the regular right-to-left approach of blockchain, where a large retailer on the right side of the value chain drives the participating companies on the left side of the chain.

The vendor spoke to several business stakeholders, evaluated the options, and picked one use case.

The agribusiness company was highly compliant with FDA and other government regulations. For example, if for some reason there is a tear in the plastic of any of the greenhouses, the agribusiness company would completely discard the produce for that time interval. The digital business vendor proposed that this practice should be monetized. How? By putting relevant details about the produce in a blockchain so the buyers can clearly see how compliant the produce is. Some of the buyers would be willing to pay a premium for such transparent and easily verifiable information.

Another suggestion was to allow the downstream buyers to see the entire chain of organic produce. Is it *truly* organic?

All this was done by first implementing blockchain within the company and then expanding it outward.

As the data captured by the blockchain increased, and because there was transparent participation from several organizations, the entire corpus of data started morphing into a single source of truth. ERP and other applications within the participating companies actually started tapping into this single source of truth for some of their functions.

Business Impact   The initiative had a tangible impact on top-line revenue by driving more orders from buyers. It also led to an 8 percent increase in margins because the company could charge a fair premium. Demand from consumers increased substantially as word spread about the company's compliance efforts. And trust improved among the players in this company's ecosystem.

2. Cloud-Native Banking Platform for Gig Workers

Pain Points

Sixty million people in the US are gig workers, facing unique challenges when running and banking their businesses. Chief among those challenges are the lack of a unified payment and reconciliation platform and an embedded cash flow management solution for the business owner.

People are not businesses, and most gig workers cannot simply accept whatever form of payment their customer desires to use. This is especially challenging for those running a gig business as their primary source of income, as it limits what customers they can onboard and consequently affects future recurring services and business revenue.

Incumbent cost structures and fees for traditional payment acceptance methods are too high, do not provide collateral value to the business, and available funds are usually delayed or unavailable without first transferring them to a nonbusiness account.

The unpredictability of income, delay in access to funds, and cash flow management challenges of nontraditional wage-based jobs presented a significant opportunity for a digital banking platform that simplifies the day-to-day management of business expenses and lowers both operational and entry cost for gig workers.

Traditional banks are generally quite unhelpful to gig economy workers in terms of savings incentives, person-to-person payment facilitation, or even proactive lending decisions based on the business's cash flow analysis.

Solution Approach

The digital enabler partnered with a start-up to solve the above issues and provide a unified platform in which workers can:

1. Accept any form of payment and enjoy an extended network of benefits they are usually denied—or are at least unfavorably positioned to enjoy—via traditional gig economy channels;
2. Access their funds immediately and benefit from higher-yield deposits and cash flow management solutions such as expense/income dashboards, direct fund transfers, and integration with digital wallets; and
3. Earn, save, and manage expenses and business cash flow from a unified bank account serving as a single source of truth for their gig business.

The digital enabler architected and built an omnichannel end-to-end digital banking platform tailor-made for the gig worker. By combining innovations such as high-speed payment settlements using GraphQL twin APIs plus a great deal of algorithmic magic, and by leveraging new bank partners to spin out real-world accounts, it was able to create a unique and value-producing platform.

Gig business clients are now engaged in a more transparent, quick, and convenient way to make payments while providing a gig-worker-friendly banking solution. The platform lies between a true digital banking solution and a business partner for the gig business owner. The digital vendor's approach enables a range of uses from registration of the gig business and payment management all the way to card and basic business banking services.

The platform provides a single source of truth as all data relevant to business operations—such as client and gig data, average transaction amounts, revenues, records of services offered, tax apportionments, or transaction history—are stored and accessible to the gig business owner. It also provides cash flow health and balance sheets. These data points can be useful in future marketplace offerings, such as underwriting decisions for a business loan.

Business Impact

- Speed: In less than four months, the digital enabler designed all user journeys, modeled business personas, architected a cloud-based digital platform, and built an omnichannel experience. The collaborative journey has barely begun, and the start-up partner is already banking hundreds of gig business owners that have pushed invoicing volume upwards of $25,000 per month from release to only a limited user base. Final customers are enjoying the simplicity with which they can pay for everyday services.

- Value creation: This start-up is generating both intrinsic value as a highly valuable, gig-economy-focused business partner and also bringing access and lowering the cost of setting up a business for those new to this fastest growing sector of the global workforce.

- Product and platform: The digital enabler's partnership extends far beyond cloud engineering services, partner integrations, custom API development, back-end services, and swiftly building and shaping a responsive web single-page application and state-of-art password-less native iOS app.

3. Digital Decisioning Platform for Global Confectionary Producer

Pain Points

A Belgian chocolatier famous for its artisanship and innovation has grown into a global premium brand over the past 90 years and now has more than 600 boutiques and presence in more than 100 countries worldwide.

The company had challenges in managing their stocks as they did not have a real-time view of their inventory. Also, they had multiple versions of products in different systems and did not have a single version across systems. There was no reporting platform that would provide an instant view of metrics such as weeks of supply across product classifications or allocations or cancellations for a specific SKU. Users normally relied on Excel spreadsheets downloaded from the ERP platform and made phone calls to validate the understanding before making a decision.

The head of customer service needed a reliable single source of data to efficiently carry out her day-to-day operations and make decisions.

The person heading the supply planning team needed to ensure a seamless transition from sales to demand to supply plan and wanted some readily available, handy key metrics for the supply chain world at any point in time.

The digital enabler team summarized the business issues they would address:

- There was a critical need for trusted information across the organization.

    Because teams at the company rely on a legacy system (black screen, menu-driven transaction system) to access data, inventory information is very local and person dependent. This leads to manual interventions in order fulfillment. The customer service team relies on Excel reports to understand the inventory position. The Excel data is one or two days old, so the team uses phone calls and emails to validate it before making an allocation.

- There was lack of data visibility, leading to manual metrics and inefficiencies.

  The supply chain team lacked visibility into order life cycle and demand by product, customer, and channel, making it hard for them to allocate customer orders. Every customer's preferred shelf-life needs are different. The lack of real-time visibility on product expiry and shelf-life changes meant it took weeks of manual effort to compute the key metrics.

- There was a lack of master data.

  There was no single product master or product hierarchies across regions. Multiple customer hierarchies were configured in different systems such as ERP and forecast and demand planning applications for different channels. This created complexity for cross-team collaboration and made it hard to infer data and relate it to sales data at lower granularity.

Solution Approach

The digital enabler team worked with the business executives and laid out a roadmap for tackling bite-size pieces. With agreement, they proceeded to build the components and run them in parallel where possible.

Master Data Management To coordinate product and customer entities that used different systems, the digital enabler created a unified master data management service in Azure Cloud that provides accurate, consistent, and complete master data across the enterprise. The data store consists of a master and several reference tables related to customer, product, and vendor entities. It provides a full audit and history of changes on a particular attribute. The team also created a dashboard to be used to steward the data. The dashboard provides information on exceptions, hierarchy definitions, and details on the create-read-update-delete cycle.

Single Source of Truth The digital enabler created a centralized operational data repository on the cloud for inventory, orders, forecast, and other transactional data. The data is sourced from multiple source systems, which are tapped to get an incremental data feed every 30 minutes. The semantics and key metric definitions are embedded in the aggregate and view layer. All collaboration and change history is stored centrally as well. This provides for a digital single source of truth replacing myriad emails, voicemails, yellow stickies, and paper documents.

Inventory Reports and Dashboards Leveraging the central operational data repository, the team layered on top three operational dashboards—one each for customer service, demand planning, and supply planning teams—and one strategic dashboard to support CXO-level decisioning. The dashboards provide an intuitive and easy way to gain insights into the underlying system. They support easy filtering across multiple categories, thus supporting the ability to slice-and-dice the metrics. Some of the key metrics are order trends, inventory trends, shelf life, fill rate, projected month end inventory, and weeks of supply.

Business Impact

- Decision making:

  Business users can slice-and-dice, drill down to analyze on a particular SKU or customer, and make decisions based on data that is available near real time and therefore highly accurate. This tool has been very helpful for customer service and for the demand planning and supply chain teams.
- Better insights:

  Having the operational data store as a single source of truth, the business teams gained a holistic view of KPIs with easy traceability from sales plan to demand plan to supply plan.
- Unlocked value:

  Business users are freed from mundane tasks of collecting information, manually extracting relevant data, and doing Excel operations. Now they have more time to focus on high-value activities related to the core business. The customer service team can confirm customer orders within minutes. Demand planning and supply planning teams' productivity further increased with automated KPI generation and one-click decision making.

- Product and platform:

   With the above orchestration of digital assets and engineering, the digital enabler was able to define and build pipelines with the governance necessary to establish trusted data stores while not affecting the ongoing business. They built reusable components that reduced the engineering efforts in multiple areas.

4. Payment Platform to Securely Scan and Classify Data

Background

The client's goal was to safeguard intellectual property and ensure compliance by protecting sensitive data associated with digital payments on premises, in the cloud, and at endpoints, seamlessly integrated with its catalog and governance products.

The client, a major payment company, owned multiple brands that cut across mobile, web, wallet, and international digital payments. Similar data elements across its different sub-brands, functions, and channels had inconsistent definitions and formats. These elements included customer personal data, confidential financial data, employment data, and intrinsic data used for authentication and authorization.

The client wanted a common model for scanning and classification that worked across its brands and was aligned with the payment card industry (PCI). The model had to cut across all of their data zones from the highly sensitive zone through to the commonly available less-sensitive data zone.

The Pain Points

- In the absence of a common platform, the business experienced complications and slowdowns in several areas: the regular risk assessment and security classification process lacked agility, because several manual interventions were required at various touchpoints.

- The client could not adopt a unified scanning automation platform, because different brands used different platforms for data stores.
- Lack of standard methodologies for data attributes in different data stores created the need for manual intervention to properly classify and protect data.
- As new information entered the data stores, there was no efficient mechanism to build the data catalog and group data elements into different classes according to PCI standards. Data stewards, data owners, and information security personnel had no visibility into the data.

Solution Approach   The digital enabler's team set out to build a model that addressed each element across all brands through analysis, design, and engineering and allowed for continuous fine-tuning of the model.

The team focused first on understanding and addressing the various adjacencies to fully appreciate the scope and dependencies.

- They held a series of workshops with individual domain teams, functional leaders, and the centralized security and privacy data reporting team to arrive at a common framework that addressed the client's end-to-end enterprise needs.
- They researched and built consensus on adopting industry-wide data patterns. Those patterns include global markets and diverse regulatory environments as well as adjacent business areas the client could

expand into and potential future partnerships. Adopting these patterns will allow the client to expand in the future without having to change its models.

The team then built a platform with building blocks that allow the security and privacy data reporting team to easily detect any impacts on sensitive and personal data elements across enterprise data stores and visualize the impacts.

They created a single source of truth that would lay the groundwork to enable autonomous detection and eliminate human dependency (and potential error) one bite-size touchpoint or activity at a time. For example, a threat and security scanner acts as a funnel for groups of data stores and automatically provides an aggregated confidence level score that determines the actions for that particular element.

The accuracy of the model was progressively improved with machine learning models using patterns from both the client environment and the industry. These were then baked into the model.

Business Impact Business benefits were realized in several categories:

- Speed and efficiency:
  - Security posture improved with increased coverage for detection of confidential data elements.
  - Visibility increased on what scanner and model versions are deployed across the organization and what classifiers are active. The process is traceable,

auditable, and can demonstrate 100 percent certainty on full element coverage for every location the scanner is deployed.

- Continuous scanning capabilities with dynamic sampling of data assets leads to enhanced security.
- Scan time on an average for 20K records is between 4 and 5 minutes.
- Metrics were generated for all the models (precision, recall, and score). Precision and recall metrics were greater than planned—more than 95 percent (versus 75 percent planned) for high confidence alerts and more than 95 percent (versus 85 percent) for very high confidence alerts.
- Business expansion was possible through seamless usage across adjacencies. System is in compliance with privacy regulations and effective demonstration of compliance with a unified solution across brands, methods, and channels.

- Product and platform engineering—the new model enables the following:
  - Extensive data store support at scale: identification of sensitive elements across all enterprise data storage technologies and in various zones at petabyte scale.
  - Integrated visibility: centralized, easily accessible visibility into findings across the enterprise for security/privacy officers, operators, and automation solutions.
  - Determination of the type of data for any element with a confidence score, and thus collected

information can be divided into groups that share a common risk.

- Simplified risk management by helping the security team assess the value of data and the impact it will have if certain types of data are lost, misused, or compromised.

- Simplified regulatory and mandatory standards requirements on PCI and improved user productivity by making data easier to find.

- Prioritized security controls and assurance that assets are adequately protected.

5. Identity as a Service: Connecting Customers for Better Targeting

Business Case

A global consumer data company wanted to offer its clients a solution that would allow them to combine anonymous data within Snowflake, a cloud-based service, using intelligent IDs the consumer data company would create. This "identity as a service" offering would allow clients to do customer analysis and create new segments without having to share customer data. When this company's team was unable to make progress on creating hash keys in Java/Python and user-defined functions in Snowflake, the company reached out to digital enabler Altimetrik.

The consumer data company had promised customers a "go live" date of November 13, 2021, which meant Altimetrik had just four sprints of two weeks each to complete the MVP.

Solution Approach

Altimetrik got involved in the following activities to build the MVP in Snowflake workspace:

- Clean Room Pre-Build (the company and Altimetrik together)

This space would be available for customers to bring their data and drop it in a designated table. The process picks the data from the customer file and generates hash keys for key attributes such as address or email.

- Customer Match View

Identifying personally identifiable information (names, emails, and postal addresses) as well as unique customer numbers on each row of the customer file via keywords in the shared data.

To create the customer view for each of the company's customers, some rules were implemented within Snowflake, such as use of Java because Python proved incompatible in Snowflake, the standardization of personally identifiable information using built-in functions and user-defined functions, and use of change data capture using Snowflake streams.

The business rules were implemented in a single stored procedure that could be executed using Snowflake tasks. The consumer-view encrypted data was used to match individual customers.

Business Impact

The company launched the project with its customers one week ahead of the timeline it had given Altimetrik. Business benefits began to show soon after launch:

- Faster client analysis and new segment creation without sharing customer data:

    Businesses were able to link PII data across different channels, different identity fragments, different identity within a channel without their identity being exposed to another party nor the data leaving the platform, and were able to perform analytics and create audiences in a private and PII-free environment.

- Faster client promotions and multichannel targeting:

  Client marketing teams were able to deploy, publish, and send audiences created in their clean room to destinations such as addressable TV, connected TV, digital platforms, social platforms, and the like, to reach out to and communicate with their customers or build their brand and customer base by reaching out to prospects.

6. Payment Platform Modernization for Large US Bank

The client is a top US bank providing institutional and consumer banking services to businesses and people around the world.

It needed to roll out new payment types such as real-time payments or instant payments in a rapid manner across the globe as central bank regulators in several countries mandated.

Pain Points

The existing payment and channels platform was supporting bulk payments and other bank transfer methods that were larger ticket size and lower volume for which the traditional two to three days for clearing and transfer was acceptable. But government mandates along with demand from gig workers to see money transfer instantaneously meant the bank needed a system that allowed high-speed transfers and was architected for high-velocity releases (one to two releases a week).

The bank hired a digital partner that would help modernize its payments and channels platform from a monolithic architecture to an always available microservices-driven, API first, cloud-native architecture. This transition to a new architecture had to happen seamlessly with no disruption to existing payments types and volume.

Solution Approach

The transformation from one architecture to another was envisioned with business domain, not just technology, at the forefront. The domain-driven design approach coupled with modern distributed system principles such as Agile methodology worked very well for this modernization effort.

The tech journey included discussions with business stakeholders to come up with business and supporting domains; setting up redundant infrastructure and software components for always-on functionality; establishing pipelines that enabled automated code deployments, quality gates, and so forth, which in turn allowed for quick incremental production releases for new features; and supporting and migrating terabytes of data from the legacy database to the target database to maintain data integrity across both systems with a single source of truth.

Simplification came from breaking down business workflows into independent services that can be scaled horizontally. The vendor provided software development kits with common functionality, which freed up the client to focus on the business problem. That approach allowed for parallel development of the user interface and back end, which helped multiple services and products hit the market together.

A single source of truth is achieved by having all the data that is collected and computed in a central data store in the platform. Because the legacy and new platform coexisted, the single source of truth is the legacy database. However, the data from legacy is replicated in near real-time to the target data store, and the new functionality is serviced through that target data store. Once all the functionality has been migrated to the new platform, the legacy product would be sunset and the new platform along with the target data store will form the single source of truth.

Business Impact

- Speed: With domain-driven design and DevOps, the release cycle has shrunk to two weeks from four to six months with the ability to make new releases with no downtime. Additionally multiple independent microservices have provided far greater business agility by allowing the business to push changes for specific functionality in isolation.
- Business outcomes: The technology platform allowed other business units that supported real-time payments in other countries to kick start their transformation without having to invest in infrastructure and base components. This has led to innovation in the way the business envisions the product working and pushes new ways to engage the customer.
- Unlock value using the single source of truth: Reporting and insights available on the single source of truth data helped business unlock value from business insights and offer innovative ways to use the product. It also helped prioritize product features based on customer feedback and insight from the data.
- Scalability and availability: The platform is cloud native, auto-scalable, has redundancy baked in, and is

available 24-7-365. This is a huge improvement on the legacy product that needed downtime every weekend to apply patches and take backups. This has greatly enhanced customer confidence and allowed the bank to garner more share of the market as well as not lose any revenue due to downtime.

7. Improving Profit Margin and Cash Flow for Small Businesses with Instant Payment

What Is the Business Need and Why Is It Important?

Small businesses face a revenue leakage of up to 3 percent for credit card fees and yet must wait three to seven days to receive the money in their accounts. Small businesses need a platform that drastically reduces fees and makes funds available in real time, without compromising the convenience and ease of use for consumers.

How Is This Solved?

Solution overview: Through the instant pay platform, consumers can present their mobile numbers or email IDs for payment instead of credit cards. The merchant would send a "Request for Payment" in real time that the consumers can authorize using biometrics on their smart phones. Once authorized, the consumer's bank would be able to push payments into the merchant's account in real time. A notification would be sent to both the consumer and merchant when the transaction is complete. At this point, the transaction would be considered final, and the merchant would receive the money in their account instantly.

The solution is agnostic of the existing system and there is no need to build a data lake.

Several different algorithms are being leveraged for authentication, request for payment service, account proxy service, and real-time money movement service.

What Does It Take to Implement the Solution?

Team needed front-end engineers, back-end engineers, cloud technology SMEs, and payment SMEs.

Duration and cost for incremental implementation is as follows:

- Initial payment prototype: 3 months and $120K to $125K;
- Complete platform development and launch for 1 merchant: 12 months and $1 million excluding license costs for directory services (e.g. Zelle) and real-time settlement (e.g. RTP solution of the clearinghouse).

What Is the Business Value Delivered?

- Improved cash flows and revenue forecasting for small and medium businesses;
- Profit margin improvements through lower transaction fees of 0.25–0.5%, compared to 3% or more for credit card transactions;
- One-touch payment approval for consumers at POS.

8. Consumer Lending Platform for Mid-tier US Banks

What Is the Business Need and Why Is It Important?

Traditional mid- and lower-tier US banks (assets of less than $20B) are rapidly losing market share to agile fintechs, which have doubled their market share in the last four years through mobile friendly and innovative digital offerings. Key problem areas for banks are:

- Inefficient manual lending processes across life cycle result in higher cost to serve loans, lengthy response times, poor customer experience, and loss of market share;
- Lack of digital loan application process with e-signatures and document uploads;
- Suboptimal credit decisions due to reliance on traditional underwriting and risk management processes with minimal use of automated decisioning and external data sources such as Venmo;
- Unable to compete in this large marketplace, traditional mid- and lower-tier banks are at risk of losing more market segments, customers, and mindshare to fintech disruption.

How Is This Solved?

Solution overview: Develop a white label loan origination system (LOS) for banks, built using Davinta assets to achieve fast time to market, with the following features:

- Integration with external data such as Venmo or Facebook for accurate credit/risk underwriting decisions;
- Mobile web and e-signing for easy and streamlined user experience;
- ML-based face recognition and identity verification for rapid submissions; and
- Integration with bank or third-party loan management and servicing systems; solution is agnostic of the existing system, and there is no need to build a data lake.

What Algorithms Are Being Leveraged?

- Commercial AI Microsoft services for ID verification data integration;
- Outlier detection algorithms; and
- Inference-based rules engine for underwriting and credit decisioning.

What Does It Take to Implement the Solution?

Duration and cost for incremental implementation:

- Building the LOS asset: three to four months and $200K–$300K;
- White label bank offering deployment at commercial bank:
  - Phase 1 deployment: six to eight weeks (for <500 select customers) and $150K–$200K;

- Phase 2 production launch: six to eight weeks and $200K–$300K.

What Is the Business Value Delivered?

- Increase lending within this fast growth segment and increase profits. This segment has decent margins because of the high rates that customers pay for these loans (average of 9% APR).
- Gain market share and improve customer base for fintech companies.

9. Physician Directory

What Is the Business Need and Why Is It Important?

For health insurance companies, managing a directory of doctors is a manual process, predominantly done by human effort through email, phone, and so forth, taking two to three months to address issues. Inaccuracies in the directory are subject to regulatory noncompliance and affect customer satisfaction scores.

How Is This Solved?

Solution overview: Develop an automated solution that would integrate data from different sources and override attributes based on source and latency of data. The solution will integrate with internal and external sources to automatically validate data on a daily basis. This would limit the data sent for manual verification by routing records that cannot be validated automatically. In addition, the routing will prioritize the records based on different regulatory needs to reduce compliance risks.

The solution will improve the directory accuracy from 60 to 85 percent, reduce manual efforts by over 40 percent, and improve cycle time from two–three months to four–six weeks.

The solution is agnostic of the existing system, and there is no need to build data lake.

What Algorithms Are Being Leveraged?

Random forest ML.

What Does It Take to Implement the Solution?

Duration and cost for incremental implementation:

- Initial proof of value (PoV): four weeks and $80K;
- Complete solution development: 12 weeks and $500K.

What Is the Business Value Delivered?

- Significant reduction of noncompliance risks for health insurance companies;
- Higher customer satisfaction scores due to accurate availability of physicians information;
- Faster, more accurate, and optimized solution to overcome manual processing and subsequent delays.

10. Virtual Product Development Platform

What Is the Business Need and Why Is It Important?

For large enterprises, business transformation is fueled by innovation to drive future disruptive changes and for SMBs and start-ups, so quickly ideating and launching solutions is extremely important. However, there is a complex world of ideation to productization—multiple steps, virtual global teams, different processes, different technologies, different tool sets, different skill sets, and so forth, all of which amplify the complexities. The lack of a standard way of enforcing and unifying the process, avoiding redundancies, and measuring productivity is challenging.

How Is This Solved?

Solution overview: An integrated and collaborative platform (a platform-as-a-service) that will enable a faster way to go from idea to product, simplifying all those idea management, application development and deployment, specialized skills, and infrastructure headaches. It will enable various stakeholders and innovators in an organization to collaborate, develop, and launch enterprise solutions to drive the business outcomes in an exceptionally seamless and unified way.

What Algorithms Are Being Leveraged?

- Digitization of end-to-end ideation-to-launch process and entire PDLC life cycle;
- On-cloud and for-cloud;

- Out-of-box support for diversified tools and technologies.

What Does It Take to Implement the Solution?

Duration and cost for incremental implementation:

- Concept and prototype:
  - Duration and cost: 12 weeks and $50K;
  - Team skills needed: Product manager and UX/ visual designer
- Complete platform development and market launch:
  - Duration and cost: 12 months with a release every quarter and $250K per release;
  - Team skills needed: Product manager, product marketing manager, UX/visual designer, and information developer, full stack developers with PaaS/SaaS experience, SaaS/PaaS architect, SDETs and engineering leads.

What Is the Business Value Delivered?

- Business innovation with faster time-to-market (quickly ideate and launch);
- Cost-effective as the ready-made ecosystem ensures faster adoption without any specialized skills;
- Unified executive insights and improved productivity of the team;
- Secure with private access, data residency, and sovereignty compliance.

11. Modern Expense Management for Commercial Cards

What Is the Business Need and Why Is It Important?

Companies that enroll into corporate card programs with banks expect timely, accurate expense management intelligence as part of the service. Banks buy spend information from different sources to meet this need. However, the accuracy of this information is only 60–70 percent, which causes dissatisfaction to the client company.

How Is This Solved?

Solution overview: The solution is to enable payment networks (Visa, Mastercard, etc.) to fill this gap. As the network operator, they have both the card information and spend transaction information. By enriching this information through tie-ups with various industry aggregators (specifically airlines, hotels, and transport, which form the bulk of all employee business expenses), our solution allows for end-to-end matching and correlation of payment transactions. This in turn is represented as intelligent spend management dashboards and reports with high accuracy. The payment networks enable card-issuing banks to meet and exceed the expectations of their corporate clients.

The solution is agnostic of the existing system, and there is no need to build a data lake.

What Algorithms Are Being Leveraged?

- Data integration;
- Matching;
- Data cleansing;
- Machine learning.

What Does It Take to Implement the Solution?

- Team skills needed: front-end engineers, back-end engineers, data engineers, data scientists, machine learning engineers.
- Duration and cost for incremental implementation:
  - Platform development and onboarding first bank client: four to six months and $800K to $1M;
  - Onboarding subsequent bank clients: one to two months and $200K to $300K.

What Is the Business Value Delivered?

- Improved customer satisfaction scores for issuing banks;
- Additional insights for issuing banks to enable tailoring of rebate and reward programs to drive higher spends on their cards;
- Ability of corporate clients to understand their business expenses with greater granularity and thereby take better, data-driven decisions on administering their employee spends.

12. Demand Forecasting and Logistics Optimization for CPG/FMCG

What Is the Business Need and Why Is It Important?

CPG/FMCG companies are unable to create reliable, accurate, granular consumer demand forecasts. This in turn limits their ability to optimize their supply chain processes across production, manufacturing, and logistics to address consumer demand in a predictable, timely manner. Inefficient management logistics lead to revenue leakages and product wastage.

How Is This Solved?

Solution overview: This is addressed in three components.

1. A platform to collect and integrate data from internal sources (demand, sales, production, and other enterprise systems) and external sources (Nielsen, retailer scan data, and social media data).

2. Intelligent forecasting models to take in the combined and cleansed data from these sources to accurately predict consumer demand for products and dynamically prioritize demand fulfilment for high-value and high-margin products to maximize business value.

3. Logistics and retailer resupply decision support platform to ensure these activities are also managed optimally to maximize availability of high-value products to consumers.

The solution is agnostic of the existing system, and there is no need to build a data lake.

What Algorithms Are Being Leveraged?

- Data integration;
- Multivariate analysis;
- Data collection;
- Matching;
- Data cleansing;
- Time series analysis;
- Predictive modeling.

What Does It Take to Implement the Solution?

- Team skills needed: front-end engineers, back-end engineers, data engineers, data scientists, machine learning engineers;
- Duration and cost for incremental implementation:
  - Initial proof of value: five weeks and $70K;
  - Complete platform build: additional eight to ten weeks and $300K.

What Is the Business Value Delivered?

- Ability to maximize sales of high-value and high-margin products;
- Higher supply chain efficiency through accurate demand prediction and optimized production schedules;

- Reduction in waste due to unsold inventory and rejected deliveries;
- Cost reduction through more effective negotiations with logistics providers and resupply windows that leverage lean periods.

13. Targeted Marketing Campaign for P2P Lenders

What Is the Business Need and Why Is It Important?

Lending companies need to focus their marketing spend on potential corporations that will respond to loan campaigns and would likely not default on their payments.

Goodwill is an important asset in the lending business. So, in addition to targeted marketing campaigns on potential customers, the companies would need to refrain from sending marketing campaigns to customers who are not likely to respond at that time (spam prevention).

How Is This Solved?

Solution overview: The solution is to collect relevant data about the potential businesses from credit bureaus and business/stakeholder data aggregators and merge that data with the historical campaign data within the company. This data can then be analyzed to cherry-pick potential borrowers.

In order to reduce the up-front capital expenditure and to obtain quick iterative business gains, the preferred approach would be to use a suitable cloud provider for hosting the solution.

Additionally, the solution will calculate the approximate loan amount the potential customers will require and can repay.

The solution is agnostic of the existing system, and there is no need to build a data lake.

What Algorithms Are Being Leveraged?

- Data integration;
- Missing value identification and imputation;
- Data collection;
- Outlier identification and correction;
- Metadata check;
- Supervised classification machine learning (e.g. decision tree ensembles);
- Data transformation.

What Does It Take to Implement the Solution?

- Team skills needed: back-end engineers, data engineers, data scientists, machine learning engineers;
- Duration and cost for incremental implementation:
  - Build initial prototype: two months and $100K;
  - First business use case to production: one month and $50K;
  - Subsequent two use cases: two months and $100K.

What Is the Business Value Delivered?

- Significant reduction in opportunity cost by identifying potential customers who fit the profile but were not being targeted earlier;
- Reduction in default risk by avoiding businesses that could potentially default on their loan payments;
- Improved predictions on loan amounts for customers leads to effective funds management.

14. Single Source of Truth—Connected Sales, Revenue, and Demand Planning

What Is the Business Need and Why Is It Important?

B2B companies are unable to have an integrated view of internal functions—sales, finance, and supply chain—resulting in inaccurate forecasting. Fueled by poor customer 360°, companies are not able to have data-driven demand planning and cascade it to downstream systems. These could adversely affect investor confidence, customer retention, sales margin, and revenue leakages.

How Is This Solved?

Solution overview: The solution is to build a platform that integrates data across internal sources (sales, finance, supply chain, and production), customer business priorities, and order backlog. Data analysis algorithms will be applied on the aggregated data and fed into machine learning algorithms for accurate demand and revenue forecasting. The platform can further be configured to monitor, measure, and report the business's KPIs.

The solution is agnostic of the existing system, and there is no need to build a data lake.

What Algorithms Are Being Leveraged?

- Data integration;
- Flexible rules engine for various KPI definitions;
- Data transformation;
- AI-based newsfeeds and ML algorithms.

What Does It Take to Implement the Solution?

Duration and cost for implementation:

- One time setup and implementation: eight to ten weeks and $150K;
- Additionally, SaaS fees per year: $300K (arrived based on license usage of 250 and multiyear commitment of three years).

What Is the Business Value Delivered?

- Drive accountability across sales, finance, and ops teams for their forecasts;
- Improvement in forecast accuracy from 75 percent to over 90 percent;
- Huge productivity gain—saving an average of eight hours per sales rep per month and many hours saved by finance in consolidation and reconciliations;
- Faster time to decision making (cut down forecast cycle from 20 days to 5 days);
- Identify up-sell and cross-sell opportunities and increased retention;
- Over $3M cost saves in year one by optimizing demand forecasting linked to real-time revenue.

15. Situational Awareness

What Is the Business Need and Why Is It Important?

The IT operation team in a company generally have multiple silos across their landscapes (infra, applications, and data), which result in negative impact to their KPIs—mean time to respond (MTTR) and time to market (TTM). Organizations need better monitoring capabilities and analytical dashboards to ensure availability of their infrastructure, servers, and applications and their costs optimized.

How Is This Solved?

Solution overview: The solution is to build a platform for continuous extraction of environmental information, integrate it with previous knowledge to form a coherent mental picture, and then use that picture for anticipating future events. The solution will identify, process, and comprehend the critical elements of information about the "what," "where," and "when" of an event. Data will be collected in a standardized form, using clustering and elimination algorithms to reduce noise in the incoming data and predict future events. All the relevant data is pulled into a cloud repository and analyzed, data being incrementally added as new use cases come up.

The solution is agnostic of the existing system, and there is no need to build a data lake.

What Algorithms Are Being Leveraged?

- Data ingestion and cleansing;
- Spectral clustering;
- Metadata checks;
- Variable elimination;
- Data transformation.

What Does It Take to Implement the Solution?

- Team skills needed: front-end engineers, back-end engineers, data engineers, data scientists, machine learning engineers;
- Duration and cost for implementation:
  - Platform build (includes data ingestion, standardization, algorithm training, and fine-tuning): eight weeks and $250K;
  - Additionally, cloud provider charges (company infrastructure would be used for most scenarios).

What Is the Business Value Delivered?

- Better control and monitoring of organizational assets;
- Optimization of operational spends by realigning their infrastructure assets based on predictions.

16. Remote Patient Management Services for Critical Illness

What Is the Business Need and Why Is It Important?

Patients with critical illnesses such as heart ailments, high blood pressure, and diabetes need an improved platform to access and respond to standard clinical pathways. Remote management such as use of telemedicine has been recognized as a service and expands beyond simple monitoring services by Medicare. This will help insurance companies to better predict the claims and cash flows. Large companies will require more health care touchpoints with their employees for optimized health care costs. Pharma companies will have data for extensive clinical trials for drug formulations and monitoring the side effects of approved drugs.

How Is This Solved?

Solution overview: The remote platform will aggregate data and have more touchpoints with patients for improved advisories on directing them to a clinical pathway, behavior tracking, and data correlation for improved outcomes.

Predictive algorithms would help in deciding the next course of action and provide recommendations based on their inputs into the platform. The streamlined and periodic data collection/processing would then enable the following:

- Pharmaceutical companies will have access to patients' data to test medicines and gather results.

- Insurance companies will have improved accuracies in terms of claim predictions.

The solution is agnostic of the existing system, and there is no need to build a data lake.

What Algorithms Are Being Leveraged?

- AI/ML algorithms for insights (health care and insurance platforms);
- API integrations (health care and platforms);
- Insurance;
- HIPAA compliance.

What Does It Take to Implement the Solution?

- Duration and cost for incremental implementation:
  - Base platform build: three to five months and $500K to $1M;
  - Complete platform as a white label product: 8–12 months and $1M to $2M.
- Available as a white label product or as subscription services to insurance, health-care providers, and pharmaceutical companies (any customizations required will be incorporated to the platform on a case-by-case basis).

What Is the Business Value Delivered?

- Individual patients will be monitored better;
- Better information at hand for decision making;

- For health care providers, one-stop solution to provide remote support for telemedicine;
- For insurance providers, increased accuracy for prediction of medical claims;
- Pharmaceutical companies will have increased access to patients' data so that they can improve their testing and create new drug formulas.

17. Mobile Apps for SMBs in Health-Care Network

What Is the Business Need and Why Is It Important?

Customers of health-care companies look for a digital experience across the life cycle of health care. The life cycle has a lot of small businesses that do not have a digital presence, such as independent clinics and small distributors.

How Is This Solved?

The solution is to build white label mobile apps and a back-end platform with approach steps:

- Building white label applications that will enable patients to book, cancel/reschedule appointments, message their dentists, update insurance, make payments, upload receipts for claim processing, etc.;
- Building a back-end platform that will send push notifications to patients to manage their appointments, remind them of their payments, process the payments, send offers, and keep them engaged;
- Building an admin portal for these SMBs to onboard and manage their account.

The solution is agnostic of the existing system, and there is no need to build a data lake.

What Algorithms Are Being Leveraged?

- Application build factory (build mobile applications in a matter of minutes);
- Conversational bots;
- Notifications design;
- Pattern;
- Human-centric design;
- Next best action;
- Scheduling algorithms (appointment management).

What Does It Take to Implement the Solution?

- Team skills needed: front-end engineers, back-end engineers, UX engineers, product manager;
- Duration and cost for incremental implementation:
  - Build a prototype: 1 month and $100K;
  - Put the first use case into production: 6 months and $600K;
  - Additionally, cloud provider charges to host the back-end platform APIs.
- Note: Apple's push notification service and Google's cloud messaging for notifications are free.

What Is the Business Value Delivered?

- Customer gets an end-to-end digital experience;
- SMBs would be enabled with instant payment collection capability;
- Efficient and higher rate of patient intake;
- Faster claims processing.

18. Incorporating Voice of Customer to Improve Customer Satisfaction

What Is the Business Need and Why Is It Important?

Retailers need to incorporate the voice of the customer/ store across product design, store operations, and so forth. The voice of the customer is critical feedback for any retailer. The feedback would help best execute marketing/promotion/price campaigns, changes in in-season manufacturing, or changes to supply to have the right product in the right place at the right time.

How Is This Solved?

Solution overview: We are taking the voices of customers from the stores and e-commerce sites, putting this feedback through language and semantic processing to efficiently group the feedback and provide it to designers and merchandisers to make improvements and changes. Over time, the plan is to bring in additional sources of data to be able to provide an even more comprehensive view.

The solution is agnostic of the existing system, and there is no need to build a data lake.

What Algorithms Are Being Leveraged?

- Data collection;
- Data ingestion and cleansing;
- Text and semantic algorithms (provide different patterns of data);
- Trend analytics.

What Does It Take to Implement the Solution?

- Team skills needed:
  - Front-end engineers, back-end engineers, data engineers, data scientists, machine learning engineers;
- Duration and cost for incremental implementation:
  - Building the base MVP to get data and basic visualization: 8 weeks and $200K;
  - Turnkey Solution Implementation: 8 weeks and $300K–$400K.

What Is the Business Value Delivered?

- Reduction of unsold inventory;
- Reduction of discounting;
- Improvement of store morale;
- Improvement of customer satisfaction.

19. Conversational Artificial Intelligence Platform

What Is the Business Need and Why Is It Important?

Vast amount of content is available across multiple industries. Mobile is becoming the primary medium for most consumers, and mobile restricts the content that can be covered. However, mobile opens a new less tested channel of conversation to get answers.

How Is This Solved?

Solution overview: Build a conversational web AI platform that would help business quickly transform their existing web content and documents into voice-accessible format.

- Create industry semantic with keywords and action words;
- Parse content to create metadata for voice;
- Create actions and skills with inputs and branches;
- Provide ability to utilize content authoring platform metadata for new content.

This can be implemented by building add-ins to web browser or utilizing the commercial Alexa/ Siri/Google/ Cortana.

The solution is agnostic of the existing system, and there is no need to build a data lake.

What Algorithms Are Being Leveraged?

- Semantic analysis;
- Semantic hierarchy;
- Data parsing;
- Machine learning;
- Conversational AI;
- Conversational UX.

What Does It Take to Implement the Solution?

- Duration and cost for incremental implementation:
  - Building prototype: 4 months and $200K–$300K;
  - Turnkey solution implementation for first use case: 4 weeks and $50K–$70K.

What Is the Business Value Delivered?

- Customer satisfaction;
- Contextualized data consumption;
- Historical data analysis (of any content).

20. Process Warehouse Automation

What Is the Business Need and Why Is It Important?

Within the process industry (especially agri-commodity processing), there are significant gaps in visibility of warehouse processes where raw commodity is taken as the input, and finished wholesale units are the output. For example, a cashew warehouse takes raw cashew nuts as the input, which go through steaming, peeling, sorting, cleaning, and so forth and come out as processed nuts that can then be packed for wholesale distribution. While ERP systems usually can track what was loaded in the farm and what is the output of wholesale nuts, they cannot track what happened in between and how efficiently the different pieces are performing.

How Is This Solved?

Solution overview:

- Enable capture of information at each step for each component from the time a load of a commodity enters the warehouse to the point where the wholesale boxes are loaded for outbound transport;
- Push this information into a data store, and enable visualization for all stakeholders (warehouse supervisor, head office business personnel, engineering, and machinery managers) in real time;

- Alerts and thresholds for immediate actions to be taken (for example, imminent failure events) and trends to be noted and preventively addressed;
- Highly configurable tablet app on industrial-grade tablets to unify these capabilities and operate within a potentially extreme environment (heat, dust, humidity, water, etc.).

The solution is agnostic of the existing system, and there is no need to build a data lake.

What Algorithms Are Being Leveraged?

- Vibration analysis with fast Fourier transformation API integration into retailer ERP systems;
- Bluetooth and bar-code scanning capabilities;
- Machine learning algorithms for predictive action triggers.

What Does It Take to Implement the Solution?

- Duration and cost for incremental implementation:
  - Initial proof of value: 6 weeks and $120K;
  - Complete product build: 16–20 weeks and $400K.

What Is the Business Value Delivered?

The automation solution enabled reduced downtime, improved machine and human efficiency, and more predictable warehouse throughput. In addition, this allows for traceability across the chain, thereby reducing risk of pilferage and wastage.

21. Open Account Trade

What Is the Business Need and Why Is It Important?

Banks offer trade facilitation services to large retailers sourcing goods from international suppliers through open account remittance capabilities. There is a need to reduce the manual effort in enabling these by simplifying the process of matching purchase orders, supplier invoices, payment terms, and discounts/fees in order to allow for straight through processing.

How Is This Solved?

Solution overview:

- Collect purchase order documents/data from subscribed retailers (buyers), cleanse them, and store them for matching;
- Enable suppliers to upload their invoices and capture the information contained therein to matching;
- Enrich the invoice information from terms and conditions from the purchase order to create unified payable records;
- Develop analytics and reporting capabilities to support reconciliation and spend intelligence.

The solution is agnostic of the existing system, and there is no need to build a data lake.

What Algorithms Are Being Leveraged?

- Machine learning–enabled OCR;
- API integration into retailer ERP systems;
- Recursive diffing for matching;
- Workflow management.

What Does It Take to Implement the Solution?

- Duration and cost for incremental implementation:
  - Initial proof of value: 8 weeks and $200K;
  - Complete product build: additional 6–8 months and $700K.

What Is the Business Value Delivered?

Due to the extensive manual intervention, follow-ups, strict payment schedule conditions, and wafer-thin margins, most banks cannot break even in this business when the trade value falls below $100 million per year. This means there is a large market (or sub-$100M retail merchants) waiting to be tapped if only the cost of operation can be reduced through automation and the speed can be improved through STP to give better SLA cushions.

22. Fleet Management through Artificial Intelligence–Based Simulation

What Is the Business Need and Why Is It Important?

Fleet management organizations testing fleet size and hubs to serve a new market run 10,000 trips to get an estimate for optimal fleet sizing. It takes up to 10 vehicles and $100,000 in costs to complete this test over a three-month timeline.

How Is This Solved?

Solution overview: Develop a simulation engine that will simulate 10,000 or more trips within a week that can be validated by one vehicle running 100 trips to confirm the accuracy of simulation at cost of $1,000.

The solution is agnostic of the existing system, and there is no need to build a data lake.

What Algorithms Are Being Leveraged?

- Static routing;
- Priority queue.

What Does It Take to Implement the Solution?

- Duration and cost for incremental implementation:
  - The proof of value (PoV) phase will take 4 weeks and $150K;
  - The complete solution implementation will take 6 months and $2M.

What Is the Business Value Delivered?

- Reduce cost of determining autonomous vehicle fleet size;
- Reduce testing from 3 months to a week;
- Accelerate time to market.

23. Digital Shopping Experience for Home Décor through Augmented Reality

What Is the Business Need and Why Is It Important?

Customers buying home décor or furniture are challenged in deciding the color, size, aesthetics, and so forth, especially while buying online. Statistics say that 30 percent of all products ordered online are returned as compared to brick-and-mortar stores, for which returns are less than 10 percent. Merchants are challenged with cost of returns, cost of quality checks, cost of inventory, and so forth. Another issue is not meeting the customer expectations and the resulting damage to brand image and customer loyalty.

How Is This Solved?

Solution overview: Build a software platform in the augmented reality space, which can be used by the business in the space of home décor and home furniture to create a realistic experience for their buyers. The software platform allows customers to take pictures of the room where the décor is needed or where the furniture would be placed. Our software would build the room/house virtually based on its dimensions while taking the picture. The décor items or furniture can be now placed in the virtual room/house to check suitableness. Additionally, the platform will show specifications of the product and also comparable products to enable and enhance customer decision making.

The solution is agnostic of the existing system, and there is no need to build a data lake.

What Algorithms Are Being Leveraged?

- Augmented reality;
- Data transformation;
- 3D imaging;
- Machine learning;
- Statistical models (survival analysis).

What Does It Take to Implement the Solution?

- Team skills needed:
  - front-end engineers, back-end engineers, data engineers, data scientists.
- Duration and cost for incremental implementation:
  - Mobile app to create virtual room and furniture fitment: 4 months and $120K;
  - Creating analytics and feedback mechanism: 6–8 months and $250K.

Additionally, AR licenses based on usage. After that, the platform would be turnkey in 15 months.

What Is the Business Value Delivered?

- Enhance the customer digital experience;
- Reduce return rate and product damage;
- Analytics can improve customer experience based on return reasons;
- Cash savings from inventory;
- Accurate inputs for manufacturing including size, quality, and color.

24. Digital Marketing-Driven Sales at Institutional Fund Managers

What Is the Business Need and Why Is It Important?

B2B wealth management advisors (around 120,000 in the US) are the target market for institutional fund companies such as Putnam. Institutional fund managers' sales approach is based on high-touch and in-person engagement, which is not a scalable approach, especially in a post-COVID world.

B2B advisors need instant access to actionable information, content, and research to better engage with their clients, make the right purchase decisions for managing that wealth, and build their client portfolios.

How Is This Solved?

Solution overview: Digital Marketing transformation will enable fund managers to evolve to more of a self-service advisor sales model.

The solution will enable investment companies to provide the information in a channel of advisor choice and with readily consumable data to drive the advisor's investment decision.

Data would be collected from digital inbound marketing channels such as fund visualizer, webinars, voice of advisors, and social media, enriched with internal data about the advisor's retention, fund renewal, and so forth. Analytics would provide the right data for the advisor with suggested actions through the channel of choice.

RIA engagement is personalized and targeted based on advisor's interests and investment company funds, which enables intelligent lead nurturing. This leads to improved marketing conversion outcomes.

The solution is agnostic of the existing system and there is no need to build a data lake.

What Algorithms Are Being Leveraged?

- Data integration;
- Data collection;
- Sentiment analysis;
- Next-best-action algorithm;
- Portfolio performance optimization;
- Missing value and optimal selection imputation.

What Does It Take to Implement the Solution?

- Team skills needed:
  - Front-end engineers, back-end engineers, data engineers, data scientists;
- Duration and cost for incremental implementation:
  - Initial discovery: 3 weeks and $50K;
  - AI/ML marketing implementation: 12 weeks and $300K–$700K;
  - Voice of customer and customer lifetime value: 4–6 weeks and $150K–$200K;
  - Tools rationalization: 2–3 weeks and $100K.

What Is the Business Value Delivered?

- Increase marketing outcomes and marketing-driven sales, which are currently only 3–4% of the overall $24B gross sales;
- Increase ROMI (return on marketing investment), marketing efficiencies, and reduce license costs;
- Enable digital transformation of the organization— move from the current in-person sales approach and emphasize digital marketing in a post-COVID world.

25. Payment Network Interchange Fees Revenue Leakage

What Is the Business Need and Why Is It Important?

The payment network clearing process has a lot of manual process to address invalid/fraudulent submissions by acquirers/merchants for preferential interchange fees. The process results in significant loss of revenue and margin. Additionally, the manual process of operational/risk teams to "claw back" revenue is expensive. The whole activity reduces the integrity of the payment network.

How Is This Solved?

Solution overview: The solution is an AI/ML application that will be used across the payment network to autodetect and flag fraudulent transactions and will feed into the business workflow for remediation by risk and operational teams.

The solution is agnostic of the existing system, and there is no need to build a data lake.

What Algorithms Are Being Leveraged?

- Outlier detection with machine learning using multivariate Gaussian distribution;
- Markov state analysis to detect pattern anomalies;
- Rule engine;
- Clustering/segmentation visualization with KPIs.

What Does It Take to Implement the Solution?

- Team skills needed:
  - Front-end engineers, back-end engineers, data
  - engineers, data scientist.
- Duration and cost for incremental implementation:
  - Initial discovery and POC: 2 months and $100K–$150K;
  - Production deployment and usage by one risk/op team: 2–3 months and $200K–$250K;
  - Scaled deployment across multiple (5+) teams: 2–3 months and $200k–$250K.

What Is the Business Value Delivered?

- Increased revenues and margin by flagging invalid transactions during settlement;
- Reduced manual processes by risk/ops teams;
- Maintain the integrity and trust of the payment network ecosystem.

26. Rapid Medi-Claim Authorization Platform

What Is the Business Need and Why Is It Important?

There is a need to convert the current analog systems that connect insurance companies and Medicare authorities on to a modern digital platform to ensure rapid processing of claims, obtain authorization, and cascade it to health-care providers so that the individuals can get treated instantly.

How Is This Solved?

Solution overview: A digital authorization platform is required to transform the existing systems that handle information the analog way for quick approvals of Medicare claims. In the current situation, the number of Medicare claims are soaring, and the current platform has challenges to support the timely needs of patients. This platform will aggregate the data collected from multiple individuals and send it across to the Medicare authorities. The platform shall validate the claims before sending it across to authorities. The authorities had to do a quick review and provide their decisions (approve/reject), which are then passed on to the health-care providers so that they can provide treatment to the patients instantly.

Solution is agnostic of the existing system, and there is no need to build a data lake.

What Algorithms Are Being Leveraged?

- Authentication;
- OCR;
- Data aggregation;
- Risk decisioning;
- Data cleansing;
- Streaming;
- Image recognition;
- Standard analytics automated workflows.

What Does It Take to Implement the Solution?

- Team skills needed:
  - Front-end engineers, back-end engineers, data engineers, insurance SMEs, health-care SMEs;
- Duration and cost for incremental implementation:
  - Discovery: 2–3 weeks;
  - Initial payment prototype: 4–6 weeks and $100K;
  - Image recognition and OCR: 4–6 weeks and $250K;
  - Risk decisioning: 4–6 weeks and $250 K
  - Analytics: 4–6 weeks and $250K.

What Is the Business Value Delivered?

- For mid-sized insurance companies, it will help process a lot of claims in a timely manner and help capture a considerable market share during this period.
- Patients will get faster approvals (along with co-pay details) and receive treatments as quickly as possible.
- Health-care providers will get their claims settled immediately along with co-pay information.

About the Authors

Ram Charan is a world-renowned business advisor, author, and speaker who has spent the past 40 years working with many top companies, CEOs, and boards of our time. *Fortune* magazine has called him "the most influential consultant alive." Companies he has advised include Toyota, Bank of America, Key Bank, ICICI Bank, Aditya Birla Group, Novartis, Max Group, Yildiz Holdings, UST Global, Humana, and Matrix.

Ram is known for cutting through the complexity of running a business in today's ever-changing environment and providing actionable real-world solutions—the kind of advice you can use Monday morning.

He began his business education early in his life working in the family shoe shop in northern India. When he took an engineering job in Australia, his bosses recognized his business talent and encouraged him to develop it. He went on to earn MBA and doctorate degrees from Harvard Business School, where he graduated with high distinction and was a Baker Scholar.

Ram has written over 30 books that have sold more than 4 million copies in more than a dozen languages. Three were *Wall Street Journal* bestsellers, and *Execution*, co-authored with former Honeywell CEO Larry Bossidy, spent more than 150 weeks on the *New York Times* bestseller list.

He teaches up-and-coming business leaders through in-house executive education programs and has won several awards for his teaching. He has coached dozens of leaders who became CEOs.

Ram is a Distinguished Fellow of the National Academy of Human Resources and has served on the Blue Ribbon Commission on Corporate Governance.

***

Raj Vattikuti is a serial entrepreneur and philanthropist who has been dedicated to solving business challenges through innovative solutions for over three decades. Raj has an innate ability to understand the changing landscape that businesses face and adeptly cuts through the complexity by providing groundbreaking solutions that simplify business models using data and technology. With a focus on digital business, Raj has used his customer-focused mindset to transform clients' businesses.

In 1985, Raj founded Complete Business Solutions to help companies solve difficult business challenges that other firms avoided. It was later renamed Covansys and listed on NASDAQ. Raj sold the business in 2007 for $1.3 billion, by which time it had grown from five employees to 8,000. Other successful business ventures founded by Raj include Synova Inc., Vattikuti Technologies, Vattikuti Ventures, Davinta Technologies, and most recently Altimetrik, in 2012.

Raj has worked with large enterprises, midsize companies, and start-ups throughout his career, and he has a deep understanding of the complexities and challenges they face. This was the catalyst for starting Altimetrik, whose focus is on simplifying business, eliminating the silos, creating a single source of truth (SSOT), and sparking innovation to realize unlimited opportunities. Utilizing practitioners, who take a business view, the company helps clients develop solutions that achieve tangible results and growth with speed. Altimetrik has grown into a pure-play digital business and digital technology transformation company, partnering with dozens of clients across the globe with over 5,000 practitioners spanning 18 offices and development centers worldwide.

Raj was recognized as a 2020–2021 Entrepreneurship and Innovation Hall of Fame Inductee at Wayne State University, acknowledged as an EY Entrepreneur of The Year® 2020 National Award winner, and was the Michigan and Northwest Ohio regional award winner. He is the recipient of the TiE Detroit 2017 Lifetime Achievement Award, 2007 Woodrow Wilson Award for Corporate Citizenship, 2002 Ellis Island Medal of Honor, and Dykema Gossett 2001 Lifetime Achievement Award and holds an honorary doctorate in business administration from Bryant College.

Raj believes in giving back to the communities he lives and works in. That is why he started the Vattikuti Foundation with his wife, Padma, to support cancer research and treatment programs at Henry Ford Hospitals (Vattikuti Urology Institute) and Beaumont Hospitals (Vattikuti Digital Breast Imaging Center) in Michigan. The Vattikuti Urology Institute offers the most advanced treatments for prostate cancer, kidney disease, bladder cancer, and other urologic diseases surpassing 10,000 robotic procedures used by urologic surgeons around the world. He also founded the Poverty Alleviation and Development initiative focused on health, education, and employment in rural India.